A History of MARKET DOWNTURNS: BEAR MARKET, FINANCIAL STRATEGIES AND PROFITS.

TABLE OF CONTENT

Content	Page
Title Page	1
Table of Content	2
Book Outline	3
Abstract	4
Chapter One: Market	6
Chapter Two: Market Downturn	17
Chapter Three: Bear Market	27
Chapter Four: Financial Strategies	42
Chapter Five: Profits	55

BOOK OUTLINE

Chapter One: Market

-Definition

-History

-Example

-Types

-Uses of Each Type

Chapter Two: Market Downturn

-Literal Meaning

-Meaning in the financial world

-History of Market Downturns

-Types of Market Downturns

-Characteristics of Types of Market Downturns

-General Effects of Market Downturns

Chapter Three: Bear Market

-Introduction for a common man

-Introduction for the financial world.

-Popular Bear Markets

-Past Bear Markets

-Financial and Economic Implication of Bear Market.

Chapter Four: Financial Strategies

-Financial Strategies definition for a common man

Financial Strategies definition for the financial world

-Financial Strategies for market downturns

-Financial Strategies for Bear Market

-Financial Strategies for Market Participants

Chapter Five: Profits

-Introduction for a common man

Introduction for the financial world

How profit is made by using different financial strategies during the bear market

Why x/y/z does or does not make profit during the financial downturn.

ABSTRACT

This book explains a lot about market -history, types, examples and uses of this market in relation to the participants of this system. It further then describes market downturns and several other events that happened in the course of a downturn from the past to the present. This book also sheds more about Bear market -Bear market being different from Bull market in various ways and popular, past bear markets with their financial and economic implications.

Also in this book are financial strategies taken in a bear market, market downturn and for market participants as well as the meaning of profits to the financial world -gross, operating and net profit.

CHAPTER ONE
1.0: MARKET
1.1 Definition:

According to most, A Market is any point where people meet to exchange goods and rendered services. It is a relationship between two parties in which money is used for the purchase of goods from a seller by a buyer and for services given. In the financial world, Markets are institutions in the economy of a country whereby parties engage in the exchange of commodities. In a market, parties may either exchange goods and services by barter i.e. the provision of a limited resource to either of the parties or sellers offering goods and services in exchange for money by the buyers.

Markets can therefore be simply defined as a process where there is the establishment of the price of goods and services. Markets allows these goods and services to be evaluated and priced, facilitate trade and enable distribution and allocation of resources in the society.

The emergence of a market place may occur in a more or less spontaneous way or rather a result of human interaction in the exchange of goods and services may construct it. However, there are certain principles that hold a market in place – these include established rules and customs, source of goods for sale, competitive pricing, booth fee, custom dues etc. In a market system, transaction occurs which involves the exchange of goods and services with or without money. There are variations in the market such as products (good and services) or factors (labor and capital) sold, selling process, taxes, product differentiation, government regulation, duration, size, concentration, legal procedures, liquidities, relativity prices, duration, minimum wages, geographic extension etc. The geographic location of a market is of considerable importance. In economics, there is national and mainstream economies; national economies can be categorized into developed market and developing market. Mainstream economies see the market as a structure that gives buyers and sellers the opportunity to exchange any type of commodity.

1.2 History:

The practice of a market has been known for millions of years but the study of history of marketing emerged in the early twentieth century. The history of marketing is distinguished into 2 phases by marketers; a.) The history of marketing practice b.) The history of marketing thought.

a.) The history of marketing practice: this is an investigation into which various ways marketing has been practiced and how these practices have been avoided over time as a response to change in socio-economic conditions. It is based on economic management and marketing strategies.

b.) The history of marketing thought: this is an examination of the strategies marketing has been studied and thought. It is based in cultural and economic history.

Two different fields of study are applied but they cut each other at different junctures. Many historians of marketing have undertaken considerable investigations into the emergence of market practice, yet there is little contention about when everything all started. Some researchers are of the argument that marketing practices can be found in antiquity while others suggest that modern marketing emerged in conjunction with the rise of consumer culture in seventeenth and eighteenth century Europe. While yet other researchers suggest that modern marketing was only realized in the decades following an industrial evolution in Britain where it was spread to Europe and North America.

Hollander and many others suggested that the controversy in which follows the different dates for the emergence of the market. It can be explained by problems which follows the various way marketing has been defined -as reference to 'modern marketing' as a planned, programmed repertoire of professional practice including activities such as segmentation, product differentiation, positioning and marketing communications and 'marketing' as a simple form distribution and exchange.

1.3: Examples of Market:

- Corn Exchange in London, circa 1809
- A market in Râmnicu Vâlcea by Amedeo Preziosi
- Cabbage market by Václav Malý

1.4: Types of Market:

Markets of varying types come into emergence spontaneously whenever a party has an interest in a good or service that another party can provide. There can be market for chewing gums in a playground; there can be market for cigarettes in correctional facilities as well as contracts for the future delivery of any commodity. In addition, there can be 'black markets', which refers to when an illegal good is exchanged, an example is markets for goods under a command economy despite pressure to repress them and another is 'virtual markets' such as eBay in which there is no physical interaction during negotiation between buyers and sellers. A market can be structured as an auction, a private electronic market, a commodity wholesale market, a shopping center, a complex institution such as a stock market and an informal discussion between two individuals.

Markets operate as systems and systems have structure. The structure of a well-functioning market is expressed by the theory of perfect competition. Well-functioning markets of the real world are never perfect, but there are basic structural characteristics that can be approximated for real world markets, examples are listed below:

i. Many petty buyers and sellers
ii. An equal access to information by buyers and sellers
iii. Comparable product.

Markets vary in form, scale (volume and geographic reach), location and types of participants as well as the types of goods and services traded. The following is a list of a market/ types of a market that is non-exhaustive. These are:

Physical Consumer Markets

i. Physical Business Markets
ii. Non-Physical Markets
iii. Financial Markets
iv. Unauthorized and Illegal Markets.

1.5 Uses of each Market type:

Physical Consumer Markets: refers to Market largely composed by products and services, which are designed for the consumer out there.

i. Food Retail Markets: Farmer's markets, Fish markets, grocery stores, bakeries, butchers markets and wet markets.

ii. Retail Markets: public markets, market squares, main-squares, Main streets, High Streets, bazaars, souqs, night markets, shopping malls.
    iii. Big Box Stores: Supermarkets, hypermarkets and discount stores.
    iv. Ad hoc Markets: Offering goods and services for bid, taking bids and selling to the highest bidder.
    v. Used good Markets: Flea market.
    vi. Temporary Markets: Fairs.

Physical Business Markets:

i. Physical wholesale markets: Sales of commodities or merchandise to retailers; to industrial, commercial and institutional or other professional business users, to other professional business users, or to other wholesalers and retailed subordinated services.
    ii. Markets for intermediate goods used in production of other goods and services.
    iii. Labor Markets: where people sell their labor to businesses in exchange for wage.
iv. Ad hoc Markets: Offering goods and services for bid, taking bids and selling to the highest bidder.
    v. Temporary Markets such as Trade fairs.

Non-Physical Markets: most commonly known as Virtual Markets. In this type of Market, buyers and sellers do not relate in that their transactions are done online i.e. no physical interaction.

i. Media Markets: refers to an area where sets of people receive the same television and radio station offerings and may include any other media type, which includes newspapers, magazines and Internet content.
ii. Internet Markets (e-commerce): is a kind of buying and selling of products and contact people for services that is done via the use of internet.
iii. Artificial Markets: constitutes demand for something which when exposure needed for creating the market, would not exist. An example is seen in Government spending with the basic aim to create jobs instead of making another product available.

Financial Markets: deal with people who trade financial securities, goods, and value done at low costs and at prices, that reflects the simple transaction of supply and demand. There are two preferred markets by investors:

i. Stock Market: For the exchange of shares in organizations, (NYSE, AMEX and the NASDAQ are the most popular stock markets in USA.)
ii. Bond Market: in this Market, participants are allowed to buy and sell debt securities sold in the form of bonds.

Other examples include;

iii. Currency Markets: used in facilitating trades which involves one currency for another. This is often used for speculation on currency exchange rates.
iv. Money Markets: a market for trading short-term debt instruments e.g. treasury bills, certificates of deposit etc.
v. Futures Markets: refers to an exchange in which one can exchange a commodity or something like a financial instrument at a time specified for delivery at a future time already specified.
vi. Prediction: this is a type of speculative market in which the goods exchanged are futures on the occurrence of certain events, they apply the market dynamics to facilitate information aggregation.

Unauthorized and Illegal Markets:

i. Grey Markets (Parallel Markets): is the trade of a commodity through distribution channels, which are unofficial, unauthorized, or unintended by the manufacturer or producer.
ii. Markets in Illegal goods such as the market for illicit drugs, illegal arms, infringing products, cigarettes sold to minors or untaxed cigarettes (in some jurisdictions), or the private sale of unpasteurized goat milk.

In addition, a stock market, equity market or share market is the aggregation of buyers and sellers (a loose network of economic transactions, not a physical facility or discrete entity) of stocks (also called shares), which represent ownership claims on businesses; these may include securities listed on a public stock exchange as well as those only traded privately. Examples of these include shares of private companies, which are sold to investors through equity crowd funding platforms. Stock exchanges list shares of common equity as well as other security types, e.g. corporate bonds and convertible bonds.

The Stock market is divided into the bull market and the bear market. A Bear Market is characterized by a price falling and typically concealed in a general belief while a Bull Market is characterized by investors buying and being optimistic hereby-causing overall stock prices to rise. A Bear Market will be sorted later in this book.

Size of the market

Stocks are categorized in various ways. One way is by the country where the company is resident. For example, Nestlé and Novartis are domiciled in Switzerland, so they may be considered as part of the Swiss stock market, although their stock may also be traded on exchanges in other countries, for example, as American depository receipts (ADRs) on U.S. stock markets.

As of mid-2017, the world stock market size (total market capitalization) was about US$76.3 trillion. By country, the largest market was the United States (about 34%), followed by Japan (about 6%) and the United Kingdom (about 6%). These numbers increased in 2013. As of 2015, there are 60 stock exchanges in the world with a total market capitalization of $69 trillion. Of these, there are 16 exchanges with a market capitalization of $1 trillion or more, and they account for 87% of global market capitalization. Apart from the Australian Securities Exchange, these 16 exchanges are based in one of three continents: North America, Europe and Asia.

Stock exchange

A stock exchange is an exchange (or bourse) where stockbrokers and traders can buy and sell shares of stock, bonds, and other securities. Many large companies have their stocks listed on a stock exchange. This makes the stock liquid and thus more attractive to many investors. The exchange may also act as a guarantor of settlement. Other stocks may be traded "over the counter" (OTC), that is, through a dealer. Some large companies will have their stock listed on more than one exchange in different countries, to attract international investors. Stock exchanges may also cover other types of securities, such as fixed interest securities (bonds) or (less frequently) derivatives, which are more likely to be, traded OTC.

Trade

Trade in stock markets means the commercial exchange of money of a stock or security that involves from a seller to a buyer. This requires these two parties to agree on a price. Equities (stocks or shares) confer an ownership interest in a particular company. Participants in the stock market range from small individual stock investors to larger trader investors, who can be based anywhere in the world, and may include banks, insurance companies, pension funds and hedge funds. Their buy or sell orders may be executed on their behalf by a stock exchange trader. Some exchanges are physical locations where transactions are carried out on a trading floor, by a method known as open outcry. This method is used in some stock exchanges and commodity exchanges, and involves traders shouting bid and offer prices. The other type of stock exchange has a network of computers where trades are transacted with the use of electronics. An example of such an exchange is the NASDAQ.

A potential buyer bids a specific price for a stock, and a potential seller asks a specific price for the same stock. The acceptance of any asked price or the bidding price for the stocks are the two standards in which buying or selling occurs at the market. When there is agreement between the bid and asked prices, a sale takes place, on a first-come, first-served basis if multiple bidders or askers at a given price are involved. The purpose of a stock exchange is to facilitate the exchange of securities between buyers and sellers, thus providing a marketplace. The exchanges provide real-time trading information on the listed securities, facilitating price discovery.

The New York Stock Exchange (NYSE) is a physical exchange, with a hybrid market for placing orders electronically from any location as well as on the trading floor. Orders executed on the trading floor enter by way of exchange members and flow down to a floor broker, who submits the order by the use of electronics to the floor trading post for the Designated Market Maker ("DMM") for that stock to trade the order. The DMM's job is to maintain a two-sided market, making orders to buy and sell the security when there are no other buyers or sellers. If a spread exists, no trade immediately takes place – in this case, the DMM may use their own resources (money or stock) to close the difference. Once a trade has been made, the details are reported on the "tape" and sent back to the brokerage firm, which then notifies the investor who placed the order. Computers perform vital roles in business transaction, especially when it is about program trading.

The NASDAQ is a virtual exchange, where all of the trading is done over a computer network. The process is similar to the New York Stock Exchange. One or more NASDAQ market makers will always provide a bid and ask price at which they will always purchase or sell 'their' stock.

The Paris Bourse, now part of Euronext, is an order-driven, electronic stock exchange. It was automated in the late 1980s. Prior to the 1980s, it consisted of an open outcry exchange. Stockbrokers met on the trading floor of the Palais Brongniart. In 1986, the CATS trading system was introduced, and the order matching process was fully automated.

People trading stock will prefer to trade on the most popular exchange since this gives the largest number of potential buyers for a seller or sellers for a buyer and is done at the best price. However, there have always been some other means employed such as brokers trying to bring parties together to trade outside the exchange. Some third markets that were popular are Instinet, and later Island and Archipelago (the latter two have since been acquired by Nasdaq and

NYSE, respectively). One advantage is that this helps in the avoidance of commissions of the exchange. Some problems such as adverse selection is then observed. Financial regulators are probing dark pools.

Market participant

The offices of Bursa Malaysia, Malaysia's national stock exchange (known before demutualization as Kuala Lumpur Stock Exchange). Market participants involved are individual retail investors, institutional investors such as mutual funds, banks, insurance companies and hedge funds, and also publicly traded corporations whose transaction is done using their own shares. Some studies have suggested that institutional investors and corporations who transacts using their own shares generally receive higher risk-adjusted returns than retail investors.

A few decades ago, most buyers and sellers were individual investors. An example is wealthy businessmen, usually with long family histories to particular corporations. Over time, markets have become more "institutionalized"; buyers and sellers are largely institutions (e.g., pension funds, insurance companies, mutual funds, index funds, exchange-traded funds, hedge funds, investor groups, banks and various other financial institutions).

The rise of the institutional investor has some improvements in market operations which came into emergence alongside it. There has been a gradual tendency for "fixed" (and exorbitant) fees being reduced for all investors, partly from falling administration costs but also assisted by large institutions challenging brokers' oligopolistic approach to standardized fees. A current trend in stock market investments includes the decrease in fees due to computerized asset management termed Robo-Advisers within the industry. Automation has resulted to a decreased portfolio management costs which results to a lowering of the cost associated with investing as a whole.

-Trends in market participation

Stock market participation refers to the number of agents who buy and sell equity backed securities either directly or indirectly in a financial exchange. Participants are generally subdivided into three different sectors; households, institutions, and foreign traders. Direct participation occurs when any of the above entities buys or sells securities on its own behalf on an exchange. Indirect participation occurs when an institutional investor exchanges a stock on behalf of an individual or household. Indirect investment occurs in the form of pooled investment accounts, retirement accounts, and other managed financial accounts.

-Indirect vs. direct investment

The total value of equity-backed securities in the United States rose over 600% in the 25 years between 1989 and 2012 as market capitalization expanded from $2,790 billion to $18,668 billion. Direct ownership of stock by individuals rose slightly from 17.8% in 1992 to 17.9% in 2007, with the median value of these holdings rising from $14,778 to $17,000. Indirect participation in the form of retirement accounts rose from 39.3% in 1992 to 52.6% in 2007, with the median value of these accounts more than doubling from $22,000 to $45,000 in that time. Rydqvist, Spizman, and Strebulaev attribute the differential growth in direct and indirect holdings to differences in the way each are taxed in the United States. Investments in pension funds and 401ks are the two commonest vehicles of indirect participation. These are taxed only when funds are withdrawn from the accounts. Conversely, the money used to directly purchase stock is a subject to taxation as are any dividends or capital gains they generate for the holder. In this way, the current tax code incentivizes individuals to invest indirectly.

-Participation by head of household race and gender

The racial composition of stock market ownership shows households headed by whites are nearly four and six times as likely to directly own stocks than households headed by blacks and Hispanics respectively. As of 2011 the national rate of direct participation was 19.6%, for white households the participation rate was 24.5%, for black households it was 6.4% and for Hispanic households it was 4.3% Indirect participation in the form of 401k ownership shows a similar pattern with a national participation rate of 42.1%, a rate of 46.4% for white households, 31.7% for black households, and 25.8% for Hispanic households. Households headed by married couples participated at rates above the national averages with 25.6% participating directly and 53.4% participating indirectly through a retirement account. 14.7% of households headed by men participated in the market directly and 33.4% owned stock through a retirement account. 12.6% of female headed households directly owned stock and 28.7% owned stock indirectly.

-Participation by income and wealth strata

Rates of participation and the value of holdings differs significantly across strata of income. In the bottom quintile of income, 5.5% of households directly own stock and 10.7% hold stocks indirectly in the form of retirement accounts. The top decile of income has a direct participation rate of 47.5% and an indirect participation rate in the form of retirement accounts of 89.6%. The median value of directly owned stock in the bottom quintile of income is $4,000 and is $78,600 in the top decile of income as of 2007. The median value of indirectly held stock in the form of retirement accounts for the same two groups in the same year is $6,300 and $214,800 respectively. Since the Great Recession of 2008 households in the bottom half of the income distribution have resulted in a decrease of their participation rate both directly and indirectly from 53.2% in 2007 to 48.8% in 2013, while over the same time period households in the top decile of the income distribution slightly increased participation 91.7% to 92.1%. The mean value of direct and indirect holdings at the bottom half of the income distribution moved slightly downward from $53,800 in 2007 to $53,600 in 2013. In the top decile, mean value of all holdings fell from $982,000 to $969,300 in the same time. The mean value of all stock holdings across the entire income distribution is valued at $269,900 as of 2013.

-Determinants and possible explanations of stock market participation

In a 2003 paper written by Vissing-Jørgensen, He attempts to explain the disproportionate rates of participation along wealth and income groups as a function of fixed costs associated with investing. Her research concludes that a fixed cost of $200 per year is enough for the explanation of almost half of all U.S. households in that they do not participate in the market. Participation rates have been shown to strongly correlate with education levels, promoting the hypothesis that information and transaction costs of market participation are better absorbed by more educated households. Behavioral economists Harrison Hong, Jeffrey Kubik and Jeremy Stein suggestted that sociability and participation rates of communities have a statistically strong impact on an individual's decision to be involved in the market. Their research indicates that social people living in states with higher than average participation rates are 5% more likely to participate than social people that do not share the characteristics. This phenomenon also explained in cost terms. Knowledge of market functioning diffuses through communities and consequently lowers transaction costs associated with investing.

CHAPTER TWO

2.0: MARKET DOWNTURNS

2.1: Introduction for the common man.

Market Downturn to a common man refers to a worsening of business or economic activity or he can say it is a tendency towards the downward of a business or economic activity. One can also say it is a reduction or drop in the success rate of a business or economy. It simply means there is a fall or a declination in the rate of economic growth of a market which leads to having an adverse effect on the owner of the goods and services which is to be made available. Hence, it is a degrading process that results to the closure or folding up of an institution. This could be an implication of either the state of the economy of a country or the choice of a consumer for another good or services (preference) – the end point is competition.

2.2: Meaning to the financial institution:

There is no numerical specific definition for a Market downturn in the financial sector but it can be commonly mean a steep double-digit percentage losses in a stock Market index over an interval of several days. Market downturn in a financial institution is a downward shift in an economic cycle, such as from expansion or steady-state to recession. A stock market is in downturn when it changes from a bull market to a bear market which is measured in months or years. It is also called a Stock Market Crash -when there is a sudden dramatic decline of stock prices across a significant cross-section of a stock market, resulting in a significant loss of paper wealth. This is often driven and influenced by Panic and anxiety as much as some other underlying factors.

2.3: Conditions responsible for Market Downturns

One of the major causes of Market Downturns is an elongated period of risking stock prices and when one has excessive economic optimism. Another cause is a Market where the Price to Earnings ratios surpasses long term averages, and there is an extensive use of Margin debt and leverage by People participating in the Market. Other factors which might affect are conditions such as Wars, large Corporation hacks, changes in federal laws, rules and regulations and also Natural disasters of a highly economically productive areas – all these conditions have strong influence on a significant decline in a value type called Stock Exchange of a wide range of Stocks. Stocks found in this State that is Stocks that have experienced a declination may end up in the rise of stock prices for corporations competing against the affected corporations.

2.3: History of Market Downturns

So many Crashes have occurred over the years and have mostly be associated with Bear Markets, however, this not a constant phenomenon in that they don't always go hand on hand. An example is the Crash of 1987, the aftermath of the Crash of 1987 was not a bear Market. Similarly, the bear market of Japan of the 1990s occurred over often and several years and no notable crash was recorded.

- **Panic of 1907**

This Panic of 1907 is also known as Bankers' panic or Knickerbocker Crisis. In 1907 and in 1908, the NYSE experienced a three months downturn of about 50% of the previous year due to a variety of factors, led by the manipulation of copper stocks by the Knickerbocker Company. Shares of United Copper rose gradually up to October, and thereafter crashed, leading to panic also because it was a time of economic recession in which there were numerous runs on banks and trust companies. A number of investment trusts and banks that had invested their money in the stock market fell and started to fold up.

The panic eventually spreads throughout the country in which many state and local banks and businesses experienced Bankruptcy. The run was caused primarily caused by a retraction of Market liquidity by a number of New York City Banks also most depositors and investors had a great decrease in confidence, exacerbated by unregulated side bets at buckets shops. The Failed attempt to Corner the market on stock of the United Copper Company also triggered the panic. The failed attempt was recorded in October 1907. When this attempt failed, banks that lent money to the cornering scheme experienced a tragedy in runs which later resulted to the downfall of the Knickerbocker Trust company – the third largest trust in New York City.

The Collapse of Knickerbocker caused a great fear which spread throughout the City's trusts as regional banks had to withdraw their reserves from New York City Banks. The Panic was not just restricted to New York City alone but it extended across the nation as vast numbers of people withdrew their deposits already deposited in their regional banks. Further bank runs were prevented due to the actions and interventions of J.P. Morgan who pledged a large sums of his own money. And was able to convince other New York bankers to do same. This is to shore up the banking system of the city. The panic continued to 1908 finally and led to the formation of the Federal Reserve in 1913.

This shows the Impotence the Independent Treasury system of the Nation, which managed the money supply of the nation yet was unable to give any liquidity back into the Market. By November, the financial Contagion was largely over only to be substituted by another further crisis. The further crisis was due to the heavy borrowing of a large brokerage firm which use the stock of Tennessee Coal, Iron and Railroad Company (TC&I) as Collateral. However, the collapse of TC&I's stock price was averted by another takeover by Morgan's U.S. Steel Corpoartion – this move was approved by anti-monopolist President Theodore Roosewelt. The following year, Senator Nelson W. Aldrich, Father-in-law of John D. Rockefeller, Jr., instituted and he chaired a commission to investigate the crisis and propose future solutions which resulted to the Creation of the Federal Reserve System.

-Wall Street Crash of 1929

The economy had been growing for most of the Roaring Twenties. It was a technological golden age, as innovations such as the radio, automobile, aviation, telephone, and the power grid were deployed and adopted. Companies that had pioneered these advances, like Radio Corporation of America (RCA) and General Motors, saw their stocks soar.

Financial corporations also performed a good work, as Wall Street bankers floated mutual fund companies (then known as investment trusts) like the Goldman Sachs Trading Corporation. Investors were infatuated with the returns available in the stock market, especially by the use of leverage through margin debt.

On August 24, 1921, the Dow Jones Industrial Average stood at a value of 63.9. By September 3, 1929, it had risen more than six-fold, touching 381.2. It could not regain this level for another 25 years. By the summer of 1929, it was clear that the economy was contracting, and the stock market went through a series of unstable price declines. These declines fed investor nervousness, and events came to a head-on October 24, 28, and 29 (known respectively as Black Thursday, Black Monday, and Black Tuesday).

On Black Monday, the Dow Jones Industrial Average fell 38.33 points to 260, a drop of 12.8%. The deluge of selling overwhelmed the ticker tape system that normally gave investors the current prices of their shares. Telephone lines and telegraphs were clogged and were unable to cope. This information vacuum only led to more fear and panic. The technology of the New Era, previously much celebrated by investors, now served to worsen their suffering.

The following day, Black Tuesday, was a day of chaos and much Catastrophe. Forced to liquidate their stocks because of margin calls, overextended investors flooded the exchange with sell orders. The Dow fell 30.57 points to close at 230.07 on that day. The glamour stocks of the age saw their values plummet. Across the two days, the Dow Jones Industrial Average has a drop of 23%.

By the end of the weekend of November 11, the index stood at 228, a cumulative drop of 40% from the September high. The markets rallied in succeeding months, but it was a temporary recovery which led unsuspecting investors into further and more losses. The Dow Jones Industrial Average lost 89% of its value before finally bottoming out in July 1932. The crash was followed by the Great Depression, the worst economic crisis of modern times, which plagued the stock market and Wall Street throughout the 1930s.

-October 19, 1987

DJIA (19 July 1987 through 19 January 1988).

The mid-1980s were a time of strong economic optimism. From August 1982 to its peak in August 1987, the Dow Jones Industrial Average (DJIA) grew from 776 to 2722. The rise in market indices for the 19 largest markets in the world averaged 296 percent during this period. The average number of shares traded on the NYSE had risen from 65 million shares to 181 million shares.

The crash on October 19, 1987, a date that is also known as Black Monday, was the climactic culmination of a market decline that had begun five days earlier before on October 14. The DJIA fell 3.81 percent on October 14, followed by another 4.60 percent drop on Friday, October 16. On Black Monday, the Dow Jones Industrials Average plummeted 508 points, losing 22.6% of its value in one day. The S&P 500 dropped 20.4%, falling from 282.7 to 225.06. The NASDAQ Composite lost only 11.3%, not because of restraint on the part of sellers, but because the NA SDAQ market system failed. Deluged with sell orders, many stocks on the NYSE faced trading halts and delays. Of the 2,257 NYSE-listed stocks, there were 195 trading delays and halts during the day. The NASDAQ market fared much worse. Because of its reliance on a "market making" system that allowed market makers to withdraw from trading, liquidity in NASDAQ stocks dried up. Trading in many stocks encountered a pathological condition where the bid price for a stock exceeded the ask price. These "locked" conditions severely curtailed trading. On October 19, trading in Microsoft shares on the NASDAQ lasted a total of 54 minutes.

The Crash was the greatest single-day loss that Wall Street had ever suffered in continuous trading up to that point. Between the start of trading on October 14 to the close on October 19, the DJIA lost 760 points, a decline of over 31 percent.

The 1987 Crash was a worldwide phenomenon. The FTSE 100 Index lost 10.8% on that Monday and a further 12.2% the following day. In the month of October, all major world markets declined substantially. The least affected was Austria (a fall of 11.4%) while the most affected was Hong Kong with a drop of 45.8%. Out of 23 major industrial countries, 19 had a decline greater than 20%.

Despite fears of a repeat of the 1930s Depression, the market rallied immediately after the crash, posting a record one-day gain of 102.27 the very next day and 186.64 points on Thursday October 22. It took only two years for the Dow to recover completely; by September 1989, the market had regained all of the value it had lost in the 1987 crash. The Dow Jones Industrial Average gained six-tenths of a percent during the calendar year 1987.

No definitive conclusions have been reached on the reasons behind the 1987 Crash. Stocks had been in a multi-year bull run and market P/E ratios in the U.S. were above the post-war average. The S&P 500 was trading at 23 times earnings, a postwar high and well above the average of 14.5 times earnings. Herd behavior and psychological feedback loops play a critical part in all stock market crashes but analysts have also tried to look for external triggering events. Aside from the general worries of stock market overvaluation, blame for the collapse has been apportioned to such factors as program trading, portfolio insurance and derivatives, and prior news of worsening economic indicators (i.e. a large U.S. merchandise trade deficit and a falling U.S. dollar, which seemed to imply future interest rate hikes).

One of the consequences of the 1987 Crash was how the circuit breaker or trading curb was introduced on the NYSE. Based upon the idea that a cooling off period would help dissipate investor panic, these mandatory market shutdowns are triggered whenever a large pre-defined market decline occurs during the trading day.

-Crash of 2008–2009

The collapse of Lehman Brothers was a symbol of the Crash of 2008

OMX Iceland 15 closing prices during the five trading weeks from September 29, 2008 to October 31, 2008. On September 16, 2008, failures of massive financial institutions in the United States, due primarily to exposure to packaged subprime loans and credit default swaps issued to insure these loans and their issuers, rapidly devolved into a global crisis. This resulted in a number of bank failures in Europe and sharp reductions in the value of stocks and commodities worldwide. The failure of banks in Iceland resulted in a devaluation of the Icelandic króna and threatened the government with bankruptcy. Iceland obtained an emergency loan from the International Monetary Fund in November. In the United States, 15 banks failed in 2008, while several others were rescued through government intervention or acquisitions by other banks. On October 11, 2008, the head of the International Monetary Fund (IMF) warned that the world financial system was teetering on the "brink of systemic meltdown". The economic crisis caused countries to close their markets temporarily. On October 8, the Indonesian stock market halted trading, after a 10% drop in one day.

The Times of London reported that the meltdown was called the Crash of 2008, and older traders were comparing it with Black Monday in 1987. The fall that week of 21% compared to a 28.3% fall 21 years earlier, but some traders were saying it was worse. "At least then it was a short, sharp, shock on one day. This has been relentless all week." Business Week also referred to the crisis as a "stock market crash" or the "Panic of 2008."

From October 6–10 the Dow Jones Industrial Average (DJIA) closed lower in all five sessions. Volume levels were record-breaking. The DJIA fell over 1,874 points, or 18%, in its worst weekly decline ever on both a points and percentage basis. The S&P 500 fell more than 20%. The week also set 3 top ten NYSE Group Volume Records with October 8 at #5, October 9 at #10, and October 10 at #1.

Having been suspended for three successive trading days (October 9, 10, and 13), the Icelandic stock market started business again on 14 October, with the main index, the OMX Iceland 15, closing at 678.4, which was about 77% lower than the 3,004.6 at the close on October 8. This reflected that the value of the three big banks, which had formed 73.2% of the value of the OMX Iceland 15, had been set to zero.

On October 24, many of the world's stock exchanges experienced the worst declines in their history, with drops of around 10% in most indices. In the US, the DJIA fell 3.6%, i.e. not as much as other markets. Instead, both the US dollar and Japanese yen moved aloft against other major currencies, particularly the British pound and Canadian dollar, as world investors sought safe havens. Later that day, the deputy governor of the Bank of England, Charles Bean, suggested that "This is a once in a lifetime crisis, and possibly the largest financial crisis of its kind in human history."

By March 6, 2009 the DJIA experience a drop of 54% to 6,469 (before beginning to recover) from its peak of 14,164 on October 9, 2007, over an interval of 17 months.

MITIGATION STRATEGIES

One mitigation strategy has been the introduction of trading curbs, also known as "circuit breakers", which are a trading halt in the cash market and the corresponding trading halt in the derivative markets triggered by the halt in the cash market, all of which are affected based on substantial movements in a broad market indicator. Since their establishment, circuit breakers have been well altered so as to avoid both gains not sure of or through guesses and losses which might be too big to handle within the short period of time.

United States

There are three thresholds, which represent different levels of decline in the DJIA in terms of points. These thresholds are set at the beginning of each quarter to establish a specific point value. For example, in the second quarter of 2011, Threshold 1 was a drop of 1200 points, Threshold 2 was 2400 points, and Threshold 3 was 3600 points.

If Threshold 2 is breached before 1 pm, the market shuts down for two hours. If such a decline occurs between 1 pm and 2 pm, there is a one-hour pause. The market would shut down for the day if stocks sank to that level after 2 pm, If Threshold 3 is breached, and the market would shut down for the day, without consideration of time.

France

In France, the main French stock index is called the CAC 40. Daily price limits are implemented in cash and derivative markets. Securities traded on the markets are divided into three categories according to the number and volume of daily transactions. Price limits for each security vary by category. For instance, for the most liquid category, when the price movement of a security from the previous day's closing price exceeds 10%, there is a suspension of quotation for 15 minutes, and transactions are then resumed. If the price then goes up or down by more than 5%, transactions are again suspended for 15 minutes. The 5% threshold may apply once more before transactions are halted for the rest of the day. When such a suspension occurs, transactions on options based on the underlying security are also suspended. Further, when more than 35% of the capitalization of the CAC40 Index cannot be quoted, the calculation of the CAC40 Index is suspended and the index is replaced by a trend indicator. When less than 25% of the capitalization of the CAC40 Index can be quoted, quotations on the derivative markets are suspended for half an hour or one hour, and additional margin deposits are requested.

2.4: Types/Levels of Market Downturns

Prediction of when there will be a market downturn/stock market crash is a difficult task, even though certain famed individuals have made a lot of fortunes in accurately predicting a decline. However, the levels of market downturn include a high level of margin debt, an overheated initial public offering (IPO) market, a high level of mergers and acquisition (M&A) activities, bubbles and crashes and Technical considerations. The first three highlighted are also considered as possible indicators in a market topping. Every market crash that has occurred since 1929 have always brought a set of new financial regulations designed to prevent a future systematic risk, which is quite difficult to avoid and predict.

- Bubbles and Crashes
- High Margin Debt
- IPO Market Activity
- Mergers and Acquisitions
- Technical Considerations

2.5: Characteristics of Types of Market Downturns

The Characteristics of each type and level of market downturns include:

- Bubbles and Crashes: Bubbles often occur due to a rapid increase in the price of a stock or asset followed by a substantial decline. These bubbles are processes that have been around for over hundreds of years -represented in the Dutch Tulip Bubble (1600s). Bubbles are as a result of a structural shift in business patterns or much larger paradigm shift such as dot-com bubble during the late 1900s and early 2000s. Also, Bubbles can also be in response to human emotions and frailty. At the height of bubbles, it is believed that people assume there cannot be a drop and anyone who is not following the crowd has been left out all along. Apparently, some initial shock occurs to the financial system or better still, an occurrence of an inherent structural weakness. Stocks and other assets are being sold in this process. This selling moves up and value keeps getting down. This pattern goes as long as into a vicious cycle of panic selling which causes a great market declination. Only in retrospect is it crystal the formation of a bubble with an unavoidable decline.
- High Margin Debt: A high level of margin debt is used to test for growth in order to see if a market topping. Investors are allowed to buy and sell with borrowed money using margin. There was a point where high levels of margin debt intersected with stock market crashed in 2000 and 2007. Quite a number of experts note that margin debt became higher in 2015 than those previous years. Similarly, a high degree of margin is part of the reason for the Chinese stock market crash in 2015. Also, high margin debt show signs of an elated market where investors load up on stocks and try to get the money as soon as possible. This borrowed money is used by investors to buy stocks, which causes the market to go up quickly in a self-reinforcing cycle. However, stocks eventually go down at the end. If stock prices begin to fall rapidly, investors receive margin calls and are forced to quickly liquidate their positions. This often results to a panic selling as investors all flee the market at the same time.
- Initial Public Offering (IPO) in Market Activity: Another sign of an impending stock market crash can be a very great deal of Initial Point Offerings. Often times, companies rush to offer shares for investors to buy and take advantage of a strong stock market, in order to get in on the action. There was substantial IPO activity before the stock market crash in October of 1987. There were 500 IPOs that year with a record of $22.5 billion raised in capital. The dot-com bubble also had a great deal of IPO activity with 406 IPOs in 2000. In the biotech sector in 2014 and 2015, there has been a great deal of IPO activity. About 50 biotech IPOs during the first half of 2015, raising over $5.1 billion. Strong performance in the biotech sector is one of the driving factors for the bullish market during that timeframe. A lot of the activity is for new and promising oncology therapies that have gained approval from the Food and Drug Administration (FDA). Whether this high level of IPO activity is a test of a market crash remains to be seen.
- Mergers and Acquisitions: Just as similar to the IPOs, a high level of Mergers and Acquisitions can also be a sign of a potential stock market bubble. Quite a number of Mergers and Acquisitions activity were made available before the 2000 dot-com crash and the 2008 financial crisis. In addition, Mergers and Acquisitions activity has been high during 2014 and 2015 as the strong stock market and cheap debt have fueled many deals, including a number of blockbuster Mergers and Acquisitions in the health care sector. Many companies seek to improve their revenues by

buying competitors or acquiring nonrelated companies, especially if revenue growth is lagging. Some experts believe the wave of mergers in 2014 and 2015 is a sign a bull market is stalling.
- Technical Considerations: Those who use technical analysis go by a different set of tools to try and predict a stock market crash. Paul Tudor Jones predicted the 1987 crash and made over 200% for his hedge fund that year. He examined technical chart similarities between 1987 and the crash of 1929 in predicting the crash. Technical analysis may look for certain bearish chart indicators such as the death cross moving average indicator. Another technical sign of a market top is a low VIX level, also known as the fear index. The VIX is a measure of the market's expectation for volatility over the next 30 days. It is calculated using the implied volatility of options on the S&P 500. Stock market crashes coincide with rapid and dramatic increases in the VIX level. There is an extended period of low VIX levels which can be an indication the market has become too bullish and there is a low complacency by investors. The first half of 2015 saw record low VIX levels. The VIX then made its largest one-month jump ever in August 2015, and is still relatively elevated as of September, 2015.

2.6: General Effects of Market Downturns

Market Downturns end up leading to a Bear Market. This is when there is another 10% fall in the market, for a total decline of 20% or even more. They usually last for 18 months. Bear markets often occur with a recession. The economy of a country becomes paralyzed with this recession -stocks are how corporations get enough cash in order to promote business. If there is a drop, in stock prices, there is ability to grow for corporations is less. Firms not productive end up laying off their workers in order to stay solvent i.e. a drop in the demand means less revenue. As a continuation of this decline, the economy ends up contracting thereby creating a recession. Sometimes in the past, the Great Depression (the 2001 Recession and Great Recession of 2008) was preceded by Stock Market Crashes/ Market Downturns.

-What Not to Do in a Market Downturn

During a crash, don't give in to the temptation to sell. It's like trying to catch a falling knife and not buying a bargain. A stock market crash will make the individual investor sell at rock-bottom prices. That's exactly the wrong thing to do. Why? The stock market makes up the losses in three months or thereabout. When the market turns up, they are afraid to buy again. As a result, they lock in their losses. Most crashes are over in a day or two. In most cases, just keep your fingers and observe how things turn out. If you sell during the crash, there is probably no way to buy in time to make up your losses. The best thing one could have done was to sell before the Crash. How can you tell when the market is about to crash? There's a feeling of "I've got to get in now, or I'll miss the profits," which leads to panicked buying. But most investors wind up buying right at the market peak. They are driven by emotion, not financials.

-Solution

Keep a well-diversified portfolio of stocks, bonds, and commodities. Rebalance it as market conditions change. If you've done this well, then you've sold off stocks when they gained in value. If the economy does lead to a recession, continued rebalancing means one will buy stocks when the prices are still down. When they go up again, as they always do, there is much profit from the upswing in stock prices. Rebalancing a diversified portfolio is the only best way to protect oneself from a crash. Even the most sophisticated investor finds it difficult to recognize a stock market crash until it is late already.

Gold is the best hedge against a potential stock market crash. Research done by Trinity College found that, at least for 15 days after a crash, gold prices increased dramatically. Frightened investors panicked, sold their stocks and bought gold. After the initial 15 days, gold prices lose value against rebounding stock prices. Investors moved money back into stocks to take advantage of their lower prices. Those who held onto gold more than the 15 days began losing money.

Most financial planners will tell you that the best hedge during turbulent times is not gold, or any other single asset. Instead, you should have a diversified portfolio that meets your goals. Your asset allocation should support those goals. But even a safely-structured portfolio should have at most 10 percent of its assets in gold.

CHAPTER THREE
3.0: BEAR MARKET

3.1: Introduction for the common Man

Bear Market in a layman's understanding is a type of market in which share prices are falling, encouraging selling. It is from the word and the animal, "Bear" that attacks its prey by swiping its paws downwards. Hence, this is the reason why markets with falling stock are called Bear Market. A Bear Market is often caused by many reasons but mostly by a sluggish, slow and dying economy of a country. It is the opposite of a Bull Market in which the market goes either up or down. The animal "bull" is known to thrust its horn in the air.

3.2: Introduction for the financial world

Bear Market is a market in which prices for securities are rising as expected to rise. It is a condition in which securities prices fall and widespread pessimism often cause the stock market's downward spiral to be self-dependent. There is anticipation of losses by investors while selling increases. While there is no agreed upon definition of what makes a bear market, it's generally accepted that an entry to the bear market is characterized by a drop of 20 percent or more over a two-month period such as Dow Jones Industrial Average (DIJA) or Standard & Poor's 500 Index (S&P 500).

A Bear Market is different from a correction, which occurs when stock prices drop by 10 percent over a shorter time frame, usually less than two months. The average bear market lasts 1.4 years, with an average cumulative loss of 41 percent, according to data collected by First Trust Advisors. It is recessionary phase over a long period of time in which stock prices plummet rapidly. There is difficulty in stock selection -a bearish outlook is one with a pessimistic opinion.

A Bull Market on the other hand is when the general market case is positive and the stock market is greatly rising. It is a condition when a smooth economy is found i.e. Gross Domestic Potential (GDP) of the economy is rising as well as job creation. This triggers the easiness in the selection of stocks. Someone who has an optimistic opinion is known to have a bullish outlook.

Mechanisms in a Bear Market

1. What happens in a Bear Market?
2. Causes/Triggers of a Bear Market.
3. Phases of a Bear Market.
4. Bear Market vs. Bull Market
5. Bear Market vs. Correction.

What happens in a Bear Market?

Bear markets are marked by low levels of investor confidence and high levels of pessimism. As investors continue to lose confidence in stocks, they may begin to sell securities as a hedge against potential losses. This behavior result to further declines in stock prices, which in turn may influence trading volume and dividend yields. After trading activity hits a trough, it may begin to increase again as speculators venture back into the market to capitalize on lower prices. If stocks begin to gain momentum through reinvestment, a bear market can adjust and become a bull market.

Causes and Triggers of a Bear Market

Bear markets can be triggered by a number of factors. The causes of a bear market often vary, but in general, a weak or slowing or sluggish economy will bring with it a bear market. Major economic shifts, including changes to the federal funds rate or fluctuations in oil prices, can influence the development of a bear market. Instability in foreign markets and political conflicts on a global scale may also come into play. The primary concern for investors in a bear market is how losses are reduced largely. To accomplish this, many investors may attempt to time the market when buying and selling, but that's an inexact science at best. A bear market is generally considered to be over once stock prices move upward again by 20 percent or more. In addition, any intervention by the government in the economy can also trigger a bear market. For example, where there is a change in the tax rate or in the federal funds rate, it may end up into a bear market. Similarly, when the investors' confidence may also signal the emergence of a bear market. The belief of investors in something happening, makes them take action — in this case, selling off shares to avoid losses.

The following are some indicators of a weakening economy:

- Low employment opportunities
- Declining Business Profits
- Existence of several new trading lows and troughs
- Less Disposable income in the hands of the general public.
- Unprecedented changes in the Government rates or various tax rates
- Short selling or increasing use of Put options.

Phases of a Bear Market

There are 4 phases involved in a Bear Market's Occurrence, they are;

1. In the first phase, while investor sentiment and prices of securities is very high, the investors are also extracting maximum profits and exiting the market.
2. In the second phase, there is rapid fall of stock prices, trading activities and corporate earnings fall and the performance of positive economic indicators are not as expected. The confidence of investors heads towards pessimism, creating a situation of unrest and panic for investors. Market indices and a large number of securities reach new trading lows and dividend yields become very high. This makes an indication for a lot more money to be pumped into the system.

3. The third phase indicates the entry of speculators in the market with prices and trading volumes continuing to rise.
4. The last phase at a slower pace highlights further downfall of stock prices. This is said to be a point of the lowest ebb and investors start believing the worst may be over and positive reaction starts flowing in with bear markets eventually giving way for the bullish outlook to come in again.

Bear Market vs. Bull Market

1. The market is mentioned as Bulls when the overall market scenario is positive and the market performance is on the rise. A bearish market the significant market decline, typically felt after a bull market.

2. In a bullish market, the outlook of the investor is very optimistic and this is visible because those investors will be taking long positions in the market. This shows anticipation i.e. security prices will increase further and investor has an opportunity to maximize profit opportunities. Conversely, in a bearish market, the market sentiment is quite pessimistic and reflected by investors taking a short position i.e. selling a security or undertaking a put position with increased anticipation of a falling market. Hence, if the price falls below the contracted price, the option holder will accordingly book a profit.

3. The economy grows sustainably in a bullish market whereas in a bearish market the economy will either fall or not grow at a faster pace as in the bullish outlook scenario. In both these situations (bull vs bear market), an indicator like the GDP (Gross Domestic Product) performs an important role in giving a bird's eye view of how the economy is performing based on the existing factors.

4. In a bullish market, the market indicators are very strong. These indicators are used in technical analysis for predicting market trends and various ratios and formulas, which express current profits and losses in stocks and indexes and its expected movement in the future. For e.g. the market breadth index is an indicator measuring the increasing number of stocks versus those, which are falling. An index of greater than 1.0 indicates a future rise in market indices and if it is below 1.0, a vice versa condition. In a bearish market, the market indicators are not strong. In either of the scenarios (bull vs bear market), the causes are interdependent and cascading effect for the same is observed.

5. The job market in a bullish situation is very bright and there are more disposable incomes in the hands of the public in general unlike in a bearish market where the job market is stiff and efforts are being made to control expenses which occurs at a rapid pace if the situation is not improving.

6. In a bullish market, the liquidity flowing in the market is very large and investors continue to pump more funds with increased trading activity and investing in stocks, gold, real estate etc. but in a bearish market, the liquidity dries up in the system and investors are reluctant before making any commitments. The investments made during a bullish scenario are sold either preventing further downsides or holding back to them for future usage. This often results in hoarding and black marketing situations.

7. IPO activities are encouraged in a bullish market since the market sentiments are positive and investors are willing to invest more money, though, in a bearish market, IPO's are avoided since investments would not be encouraged and people will prefer to hold on to the positions and liquidity existing before.

8. International investments will automatically be encouraged in a bullish market with the intention to expand the existing portfolio. For instance, if India is going through a bullish phase and South Korea decides to make generous investments in India, such a move will encourage the smooth phase for India, enhance the investment made by South Korea and in turn boost the economy for South Korea thereby spreading the effects of a bullish market across borders. However, in a bearish market, international investments may not be a nice option for other countries and such a move could be adjusted to a date to come.

9. A bullish market will encourage the banking sector to reduce the interest rates on loans encouraging business activities to grow prompting expansionary policies by the Central Bank and the Government. Conversely, in a bearish market, the banking sector will curb the usage of money for emergency prompting contractionary policies by the highest authorities. The interest loans would be held either stable or increased.

10. In a bullish market, the yields on securities and dividends will be low listing the financial strength of the investor and security others can receive on investment made whereas, in a bearish market, these yields are very high indicating requirement of funds and attempting to lure investors by offering higher yields on securities at a later date.

Bear Market vs. Correction

A bear market should not be confused with a correction, which is a short-term trend and has a duration lesser than two months. Corrections offer a good time for value investors to find an entry point into stock markets but bear markets rarely provide suitable points of entry. This is because it is almost impossible to determine a bear market's bottom. Trying to recoup losses can be an uphill battle and hence a difficult task, unless investors are short sellers or use other strategies to make gains in falling markets. Between 1900 and 2015, there were 32 bear markets, averaging one every

3.5 years. The last bear market coincided with the global financial crisis occurring between October 2007 and March 2009, during which time the DJIA declined 54 percent during the time interval.

Short Selling in Bear Markets

Investors can make gains in a bear market by short selling. This technique involves selling borrowed shares and buying them back at reduced prices. A short seller must borrow the shares from a broker before a short sell order is placed on the item. The short seller's profit and loss amount is the difference between the price at which the shares were sold and the price at which they were bought back, which is known as "covered." For example, an investor shorts 100 shares of a stock at $94.00. The price falls and the shares are covered at $84.00. The investor pockets a profit of $10 x 100 = $1,000.

Put Options and Inverse ETFs in Bear Markets

A put option gives the owner the right, but not the obligation, to sell a stock at a specific price on, or before, a certain date. Put options can be used to speculate on falling stock prices, and to hedge against falling prices to protect long-only portfolios. Investors must have options privileges in their accounts to make such trades. Inverse ETFs are designed to change values in the opposite direction of the index they are tracking. For example, the inverse ETF for the S&P 500 would increase by 1% if the S&P 500 index decreased by 1%. There are many leveraged inverse ETFs that magnify the returns of the index they track by two and three times. Like options, inverse ETFs can be used to speculate or protect portfolios.

3.3: Popular Bear Market

The stock market has been on an upswing for a number of years, although it has been particularly volatile lately as trade war fears have heated up, suggesting that this might be the right time to consider bear market inverse ETFs. Beyond the recent selling pressure, contrarian investors consider the overall long-term bull market to be a good reason to expect a temporary bear market or a very large drop. When everyone thought, stocks are on their way up, enthusiasm can lead to values that are unrealistic. Any seasoned investor knows that the conviction that stocks won't go down is dangerous. The market is said to climb a wall of worry. Prices climb when there are people who think they won't. This balance of selling pressure and buying euphoria keeps the market in balance and avoids what can be said to be an "overbought" condition.

If you want to play a market correction or pull-back, you will need to short stocks. One of the best ways to do this is with reverse equity exchange-traded funds (ETFs), or inverse ETFs. An inverse exchange-traded fund (ETF) makes money when stocks go down in price. If the index the fund follows goes down 1%, the inverse ETF goes up 1%. Money managers achieve this by making the stocks on the index short. We have selected four ETFs for a bear market that are designed to short the market and make you money when stocks fall. The selections were made based on total assets. We did not select based on year-to-date yield as our criteria because the market has been volatile in the first quarter of 2018, and inverse ETFs would not be expected to have much of a yield in that situation.

You can put these ETFs on a watch list, and if you see bigger signs of trouble in the marketplace than the recent volatility, you will be ready to jump in and take advantage of the declination. All figures are current as of April 8, 2018,

1. ProShares Short S&P 500 (SH)

SH uses the S&P 500 as its benchmark. It aims to match the performance of that index if it starts going down. It does this by investing in derivatives. This can include futures contracts, swaps, and stock options.

The fund focuses on the behavior of large-cap stocks but also watches real estate investment trusts (REITS). Keep in mind that an investment in this fund will lose money if stock prices go up. This is a fund for the short term when you think you see a temporary decline in the market about to happen.

Avg. Volume: 6,179,552

Net Assets: $1.52 billion

Yield: 0.18%

YTD Return: 0.53%

Expense Ratio (net): 0.89%

2. ProShares UltraShort S&P 500 (SDS)

SDS is an aggressive fund that tries to achieve the double of what the inverse of the S&P 500 is. The large-cap focus and the aim of 2x the inverse of the index make SDS a higher-risk ETF than SH (listed above).

This fund is for those who are so sure and convinced that the market will experience a declination. You would be expecting to make twice as much as SH. You would also be taking a risk doubled of normal.

Derivatives from the funds are used to achieve its goals. This is a short-term play. The fund is nearly breakeven for 2018, but was down double-digits as recently as February. Note the Investors take advantage of a negative market like this with a fund.

Avg. Volume: 7,845,022

Net Assets: $836.19 million

Yield: 0.28%

YTD Return: -0.02%

Expense Ratio (net): 0.89%

3. ProShares UltraPro Short S&P 500 (SPXU)

This is the most aggressive fund on our list. It aims to achieve three times the inverse of the performance of the S&P 500. SPXU offers the highest returns of the three ETFs on our list, and it carries the highest risk. If the market turns against you, you start losing money fast as a result.

If you get into this inverse ETF, be prepared to always be on the watch daily and stay abreast of any news affecting the broader market. This fund can be used to make money fast and get out at the first sign of a market recovery. On the upside, with more than 11 million shares changing hands every day, it is the most liquid of the four funds featured.

Avg. Volume: 15,813,993

Net Assets: $448.68 million

Yield: 0.34%

YTD Return: -1.51%

Expense Ratio (net): 0.90%

4. ProShares Short Russell2000 (RWM)

This ETF is tied to the Russell 2000. You would use this ETF if you expected small-cap stocks on the Russell index to decline in price.

The fund uses derivatives. RWM is a good example of how you can invest in a way that only shorts one type of stock, while remaining "long" in stocks from another index.

Avg. Volume: 444,957

Net Assets: $301.63 million

Yield: 0.16%

YTD Return: -0.28%

Expense Ratio (net): 0.95%

In conclusion, a true bear market can last a long time. Given the current condition of the market, you are more likely to take advantage of temporary pullbacks or perhaps a correction. You can make money in these downtrends by using ETFs that deals with a broad index. Three out of four of the ETFs on this list follow the S&P 500. This means you will expect the market, in general, to turn negative for a very long period of time than the current selloff. If the market turns bearish overall, these bear market ETFs will be poised to take advantage.

3.4: Past Bear Markets

- Kipper und Wipper 1623: A financial crisis caused by debased (fraudulent) foreign coins minted in the Holy Roman Empire from 1621–1623, which generate funds at the start of the Thirty Years' War.
- Tulip mania Bubble 1637: A bubble (1633–37) in the Netherlands during which contracts for bulbs of tulips reached extraordinarily high prices, and suddenly collapsed.
- The Mississippi Bubble 1720: Banque Royale by John Law stopped payments of its note in exchange for specie and as resulted to an economic collapse in France.
- South Sea Bubble of 1720: Affected early European stock markets, during early days of chartered joint stock companies.
- Bengal Bubble of 1769: Primarily caused by the British East India Company, whose shares fell from £276 in December 1768 to £122 in 1784
    - Credit crisis of 1772
- Financial Crisis of 1791–92: 1791 Shares of First bank of US boom and bust in Aug and Sept 1791. Groundwork of Alexander Hamilton's cooperation with the Bank of New York to end this event would be crucial in ending the Panic of 1792 next year.
- Panic of 1796–97: 1796 A series of downturns in Atlantic credit markets led to broader commercial downturns in Great Britain and the United States.
    - Panic of 1819
    - Panic of 1825
    - Panic of 1837: 10 May 1837
        - Panic of 1847
        - Panic of 1857
        - Panic of 1866

- Black Friday: 24 Sep 1869
- Panic of 1873: 9 May 1873 Initiated the Long Depression in the United States and much of Europe
- Paris Bourse crash of 1882 19 Jan 1882
- Panic of 1884 1884
- Encilhamento 1890 Lasting 3 years, 1890–1893, a boom and bust process that boomed in late 1880s and burst on early 1890s, causing a great fall in the Brazilian economy and aggravating an already unstable political situation.
- Panic of 1893
- Panic of 1896
- Panic of 1901: 17 May 1901 Lasting 3 years, the market was spooked by the assassination of President McKinley in 1901, later coupled with a severe drought later the same year.
- Panic of 1907: Oct 1907 Lasting over a year, markets took fright after U.S. President.
- Theodore Roosevelt had threatened to rein in the monopolies that flourished in various industrial sectors, notably railways.
- Wall Street Crash of 1929: 24 Oct 1929 Lasting over 4 years, the bursting of the speculative bubble in shares caused the further selling as people who had borrowed money to buy shares had to cash them in, when their loans were called in; also, called the Great Crash or the Wall Street Crash, leading to the Great Depression.
- Recession of 1937–38 1937 Lasting around a year, this share price fall was triggered by an economic recession within the Great Depression and doubts about the effectiveness of Franklin D. Roosevelt's
- New Deal policy.
- Kennedy Slide of 1962: 28 May 1962 Also known as the 'Flash Crash of 1962'
- Brazilian Markets Crash of 1971: July 1971 Lasting through the 1970s and early-1980s, this was the end of a boom that started in 1969, compounded by the 1970s-energy crisis coupled with early 1980s

- Latin American debt crisis.
- 1973–74 stock market crash Jan 1973 Lasting 23 months was a dramatic rise in oil prices, the miners' strike and the downfall of the Heath government.
- Souk Al-Manakh stock market crash Aug 1982
- Black Monday 19 Oct 1987
- Rio de Janeiro Stock Exchange Crash June 1989 Rio de Janeiro Stock Exchange Crash, due to its weak internal controls and absence of credit discipline, that led to its collapse, and of which it never recovered
- Friday the 13th mini-crash: 13 Oct 1989 Failed leveraged buyout of United Airlines causes crash
- Early 1990s recession July 1990 Iraq invaded Kuwait in July 1990, which led to an increase in oil prices. The Dow dropped 18% in three months, from 2,911.63 on July 3 to 2,381.99 on October 16, 1990. This recession lasted for approximately 8 months.
- Japanese asset price bubble 1991 Lasting approximately twenty years, through at least the end of 2011, share and property price bubble bursts and turns into a long deflationary recession. Some of the key economic events during the collapse of the Japanese asset price bubble include the 1997 Asian financial crisis and the Dot-com bubble. In addition, more recent economic events, such as the late-2000s financial crisis and August 2011 stock markets fall have prolonged this period.
- Black Wednesday: 16 Sep 1992 The Conservative government was forced to withdraw the pound sterling from the European Exchange Rate Mechanism (ERM) after they were unable to keep sterling above its agreed lower limit.
- 1997 Asian financial crisis: 2 July 1997 Investors deserted emerging Asian shares, including an overheated Hong Kong stock market. Crashes occur in Thailand, Indonesia, South Korea, Philippines, and elsewhere, reaching a climax in the October 27, 1997 mini-crash.
- October 27, 1997, mini-crash: 27 Oct 1997 Global stock market crash which was due to an economic crisis in Asia.
- 1998 Russian financial crisis: 17 Aug 1998 The Russian government devalues the ruble, defaults on domestic debt, and declares a moratorium on payment to foreign creditors.

- Dot-com bubble: 10 March 2000 Collapse of a technology bubble.
- Economic effects arising from the September 11 attacks: 11 Sep 2001 The September 11 attacks caused global stock markets to drop sharply. The attacks themselves caused approximately $40 billion in insurance losses, making it one of the largest insured events ever. See world economic effects arising from the September 11 attacks.
- Stock market downturn of 2002: 9 Oct 2002 Downturn in stock prices during 2002 in stock exchanges across the United States, Canada, Asia, and Europe. After recovering from lows reached following the September 11 attacks, indices slid steadily starting in March 2002, with dramatic declines in July and September leading to lows last reached in 1997 and 1998. See stock market downturn of 2002.
- Chinese stock bubble of 2007: 27 Feb 2007 The SSE Composite Index of the
- Shanghai Stock Exchange tumbles 9% from unexpected selloffs, the largest drop in 10 years, triggering major drops in worldwide stock markets.
- United States bear market of 2007–09: 11 Oct 2007 Till June 2009, the Dow Jones Industrial Average, Nasdaq Composite and S&P 500 all experienced declines of greater than 20% from their peaks in late 2007.
- Financial crisis of 2007–08 16 Sep 2008: On September 16, 2008, failures of large financial institutions in the United States, due primarily to exposure of securities of packaged subprime loans and credit default swaps issued to insure these loans and their issuers, rapidly devolved into a global crisis leading in a number of bank failures in Europe and sharp reductions in the value of equities (stock) and commodities worldwide. The failure of banks in Iceland resulted in a devaluation of the Icelandic króna and threatened the government with bankruptcy. Iceland was able to secure an emergency loan from the IMF in November. Later on, U.S. President, George W. Bush signs the Emergency Economic Stabilization Act into law. This creates a Troubled Asset Relief Program (TARP) to purchase failing bank assets. Had disastrous effects on the world economy along with world trade.
- 2009 Dubai debt standstill: 27 Nov 2009 Dubai requests a debt deferment following its massive renovation and development projects, as well as the Great Recession. The announcement causes global stock markets to drop.
- European sovereign debt crisis: 27 April 2010 Standard & Poor's downgrades Greece's sovereign credit rating to junk four days after the activation of a €45-billion EU– IMF bailout, triggering the decline of stock markets worldwide and of the Euro 's value, and furthering a European sovereign debt crisis.

- 2010 Flash Crash: 6 May 2010- The Dow Jones Industrial Average suffers its worst intra-day point loss, dropping nearly 1,000 points before partially recovering.

- August 2011 stock markets fall: 1 Aug 2011 S&P 500 entered a short-lived bear market between 2nd May 2011 (intraday high: 1,370.58) and 4th October 2011 (intraday low: 1,074.77), a decline of 21.58%. The stock market rebounded thereafter and ended the year flat.

- 2015–16 Chinese stock market crash: 12 June 2015 China stock market crash began in June and continued into July and August. In January 2016, Chinese stock market experiences a steep sell-off which sets off a global rout.

- . 2015–16 stock market selloff: 18 August 2015 The Dow Jones fell 588 points during a two-day period, 1,300 points from August 18–21. On Monday, August 24, world stock markets were down substantially, wiping out all gains made in 2015, with interlinked drops in commodities such as oil, which hit a six-year price low, copper, and most of Asian currencies, but the Japanese yen, losing value against the United States dollar.

3.5: Financial and Economic Implication of Bear Market

During a bear market, some investors may choose to focus on two fundamental principles which allow for taking advantage of the current market situation. First, a bear market is only bad if you plan on selling your stock or need your money immediately. Second, falling stock prices and depressed markets are the friend of the long-term, value investor.

If you typically invest long-term with the intent to hold your shares for decades, a bear market gives a very great opportunity to speed up your returns over longer periods despite seeming counterintuitive. With lowered stock prices, if you make fixed-amount investments periodically over time in a stock, known as "dollar-cost averaging," you can bring down the average cost basis of your holdings and shorten your portfolio's recovery period once the bear market eases up. This way, you'll end up buying more shares when the price is down and fewer shares when the price moves up.

Additionally, if you own dividend-paying stocks, reinvesting those dividends acts as a "return accelerator." The reinvested dividends reduce the cost basis of your portfolio as a whole so the quoted market value needs to increase by a smaller degree to reach break-even than your investment's original cost.

-Change in Situation.

When buying stock in a bear market, some investors choose the methodology of legendary investor Warren Buffett, "value investing," which entails choosing stocks based on the underlying company's operational quality and ability to generate solid earnings over time. These company stocks make good long-term holds and will likely still have stable earnings 10 or 20 years down the road.

This brings up a third principle when dealing with bear markets. To take another cue from Warren Buffet, learn to separate the stock price from the underlying business. This is because they often have very little or nothing to do with each other over the short-term. Even if the market doesn't currently recognize a company's worth and undervalues its stock, if the company continues to make money as an operating business with solid financial and other characteristics, this says more about the intrinsic value, or essential nature of the company, than that reflected in its current share price.

CHAPTER FOUR
4.0: FINANCIAL STRATEGIES

4.1: Definition for the common man

Financial strategies are certain practices a firm or an institution adopts in order to pursue its financial objectives.

4.2: Definition for the financial world

Financial Strategies is an approach which is planned for the development of the Finance function, based on a clearly defined purpose, plans, strategy and roadmap. Financial strategies help to build insights from sources like business context, stakeholder expectations and own performance as well as capabilities in order to create opportunities that also create value. This is a major part of an organization's plan which has been set out with the aim of meeting the financial objectives for now and the Future.

4.3: Financial Strategies for Market Downturns

There are 8 financial strategies for market downturns. These include;

- Keep Your Fears in Check

There is an old saying on Wall Street: "The Dow climbs a wall of worry." In other words, over time the Dow has continued to rise despite economic woes, terrorism and countless other calamities. Investors should try to always separate their investment decision-making process from their emotions. What seems like a massive global catastrophe one day may be remembered as nothing more than a blip on the radar screen a few years down the road.

- Average Down Costs With DCA

The most important thing one must bear in mind during an economic slowdown is that it's normal for the stock market to have years of negativity—it's a part of the business cycle. If you are a long-term investor (meaning a time horizon of 10+ years), an option is to take advantage of dollar-cost averaging (DCA). By purchasing shares regardless of price, one ends up buying shares at a low price when the market is down. Over the long run, the cost will "average down," leaving one with a better overall entry price for your shares.

- Play Dead

During a bear market, the bears and the bulls rule don't stand a chance. There's an old saying that the best thing to do during a bear market is to play dead—it's the same protocol as if you met a real grizzly in the woods. Fighting back is a very dangerous and more gamble. By staying calm and not making any sudden moves, one is safe from becoming a bear's lunch. Playing dead in financial terms means you are putting a larger portion of your portfolio in money market securities such as certificates of deposit (CDs), U.S. Treasury bills, and other instruments with high liquidity and short maturities.

- Invest Only What You Can Afford to Lose

Investing is important but same is for eating and keeping a roof over one's head. It's not wisdom to take short-term funds (i.e. money for the mortgage or groceries) and invest them in stocks. As a general rule, investors should not get involved in equities unless they have an investment horizon of at least five years, preferably longer, and money that they can't afford to lose should not be invested at all. Remember, bear markets and even minor corrections can be extremely destructive.

- Diversify

The heart of diversification is having a percentage of your portfolio spread among stocks, bonds, cash and alternative assets. How your portfolio is sliced up depends on your risk tolerance, time horizon, goals, etc. Every investor's situation is different. A proper asset allocation strategy will allow you to avoid the potentially negative effects resulting from placing all your eggs in one basket.

- ETFs Take Stock in Defensive Industries

Defensive or non-cyclical stocks are securities that generally perform better than the overall market even when times are bad. These types of stocks provide some consistent dividend and stable earnings, regardless of the state of the overall market. Companies that produce household non-durables -- such as toothpaste, shampoo and shaving cream are examples of defensive industries because people will still use these items in hard times.

- Look for Value Stocks

Bear markets can provide great opportunities for investors. The trick is to know what you are looking for. Beaten up, battered, and underpriced; these are all descriptions of stocks during a bear market. Value investors such as Warren Buffett often view bear markets as buying opportunities because the valuations of good companies get hammered down along with the poor companies and sit at very attractive valuations. Buffett often builds up his position in some of his favorite stocks during less-than-cheery times in the market because he knows how the market's nature operates that is to punish even good companies by more than they deserve.

- Consider Inverse ETFs

Inverse exchange-traded funds (ETFs) give investors a chance to profit from a decline in major indexes or benchmarks, such as the Nasdaq 100. When the major indexes decline, these funds increase, allowing you to profit while the rest of the market suffers.

4.3: Financial Strategies for Bear Markets

There are also 8 financial strategies for a bear market, they include:

1. Go to 100% Cash: This is a drastic move and it is one that may be done out of fear and panic.

Benefit: You can let the market fall and not have a care about anything in the world.

Danger: When do you get back in? If fear and panic drove you out, seeing the market rally may entice you back in at the wrong time. Bear markets have "sucker rallies" which attracts and fool people into thinking the decline is over.

Solution: Make your decisions based on fundamentals and make the decisions on what fundamentals will bring you back in.

2. Go Partially into Cash: Selling off the most overvalued securities in a portfolio is a reasonable strategy. This requires analysis and a strategy.

Benefit: Cash is always available to buy when stocks are cheaper and the portfolio is protected during the decline.

Danger: Bear markets may last a long time (years), and investors with cash can become anxious and curious to get back in. Getting back in too soon can expose an investor to the rest of the bear which is a bad deal.

3. Use Portfolio Hedges: Some securities that can help give a portfolio some protection or a hedge designed to move in the opposite direction of the major indices. These include index options, futures, inversely correlated ETFs, and shorting. Depending on your level of skill, knowledge and risk tolerance, some may be work and give good result and some might not.

Benefit: If done well and properly, these strategies can offset some or all of the losses of a portfolio.

Danger: Since these types of securities move in the opposite direction of the market, the losses can be substantial if the market rallies. Also, shorting involves risks not limited. (At Cornerstone, we never short, but do use other tools/strategies to hedge portfolios.)

4. Stop Loss Orders: To protect a portfolio on the downside, Stop Loss orders may be the answer. It is an order placed below the current price. If the stock falls to that price, it is sold automatically.

Benefit: You can keep your portfolio until the Stops are hit, and you can increase the Stops as there is an inflation in the price of the securities.

Danger: Stop Loss orders do not guarantee that your stock will be sold at that price. Once a stock price hits the stop, it becomes a market order and is traded at the market. If the stock drops below the Stop price, you may get the lower price.

5. Employ a Tactical Strategy: This allows an investor to be exposed to various sectors or securities for the time interval that the sector or security fits the parameters of the Tactical Strategy. A Tactical Strategy may allow for the portfolio to be fully invested and may have a strategy that would go fully into cash, based on market conditions.

Benefit: it gives the investor the ability to be all in, partially in or all out of the market. It can benefit from the rallies in a bear market while having a strategy to get out when things start back down.

Danger: The strategy has to be able to actually go all cash. The strategy should not be one that stays fully invested but shifts among asset classes. No tactical strategy guarantees against losses.

6. Actively Trade: This strategy is not for all investors but very few investors. By actively trade, I do not mean day trade but rather watching a particular security and trading the same from point A to point B and not caring if it goes further up. Most importantly, a trader has to be willing to take losses if it doesn't work out right.

Benefit: if done right, it can add percentages of return to the performance of a portfolio.

Danger: Money could be lost very easily. Trades can become long-term holds if they decline and you do not have the discipline to take the loss. Also, Appetite of investors can largely increase and he can get greedy and start to get in over their heads by trading too much too often. That is when problems can happen and losses pile up easily and quickly.

7. Contrarian: Watching for the securities that have gone down the most first can be of great help if they also recover first. When the market is down 10%, a sector that is down 50% might be a place to start looking for contrarian plays.

Benefit: With discipline, it can get an investor into the securities everyone else is selling, at good and desired prices.

Danger: It takes a strong stomach to go against the grain. Be prepared to see what you buy go lower, so focusing on the long term is essential.

8. Stay Put – Do Nothing. This is the advice given to many investors as they watch their portfolios dwindle. While it is a good advice during a bull market, it may not be a pleasant strategy during a bear. Doing nothing means you are willing to accept all the risk of the market. This can't be said to be a good strategy.

Benefit: You don't have to do anything, and when the market eventually recovers, you are fully invested.

Danger: Markets can take years to fully recover. According to Dow Jones data, the Dow Jones didn't stay above its peak in 1966 until 1982. Nikkei data shows that the current market in Japan is still down more than 50% from its peak in 1989, 27 years from now, that's really a great risk!

4.5: Financial Strategies for each Market Participants

- Governments and Central Banks

The most influential participants involved in the forex market are the central banks and federal governments. In most countries, the central bank is an extension of the government and conducts its policy in unison with the government. However, some governments feel that a more independent central bank is more effective in balancing the goals of managing inflation and keeping interest rates low, which usually increases the economic growth of the country. No matter the degree of independence that a central bank may have, government representatives usually have regular meetings with central bank representatives to discuss monetary policy. Thus, central banks and governments are usually on the same page when it comes to monetary policy.

Central banks are often tasked with maintaining foreign reserve volumes and adjusting monetary policy in order to meet certain economic goals. For example, In Oman, bond sales were recently conducted for the first time in two decades to help fund deficits and defend its currency peg to the U.S. dollar. Falling oil prices and increased government spending in Oman in recent years have resulted into a rise in speculation about the future of the country's currency peg. This is sure to be one macro-level currency story that forex traders will keep an eye on.

- Banks and Other Financial Institutions

Along with central banks and governments, some of the largest participants involved with forex transactions are banks. Most people who need foreign currency for small-scale transactions, like money for traveling, deals within the neighborhood banks. However, individual transactions pale in comparison to the dollars that are traded between banks, better known as the interbank market. Banks make currency transactions with each other on electronic brokering systems that are based on credit. Only banks that have credit relationships with each other can engage in transactions. The larger banks tend to have more credit relationships, which allow those banks to receive better foreign exchange prices. The smaller the bank, the fewer credit relationships it has and the lower the priority it has on the pricing scale.

Banks, in general, act as dealers in the sense that they are willing to buy/sell a currency at the bid/ask price. One way that banks make money on the forex market is by exchanging currency at a higher price than they paid to obtain it. Since the forex market is a world-wide market, it is common to see different banks with slightly different exchange rates for the same currency.

- Hedgers

Some of the biggest clients of these banks are international businesses. Whether a business is selling to an international client or buying from an international supplier, there is inevitably a need to deal with the volatility of fluctuating exchange rates.

If there is one thing that management (and shareholders) hate, it is uncertainty or not having strong convictions. Having to deal with foreign-exchange risk is a big problem for many multinational corporations. For example, suppose that a German company orders some equipment from a Japanese manufacturer that needs to be paid in yen one year from now. Since the exchange rate can fluctuate in any direction over the course of a year, the German company has no way of knowing whether it will end up paying more or less euros at the time of delivery, this shows the level of the uncertainty.

One choice that a business can make to reduce the uncertainty of foreign-exchange risk is to go into the spot market and make an immediate transaction for the foreign currency that they need.

Unfortunately, businesses may not have enough cash on hand to make such transactions in the spot market or may not want to hold large amounts of foreign currency for long periods of time which shows it uncertainty level. Therefore, businesses quite often employ hedging strategies in order to lock in a specific exchange rate for the future, or to simply remove all exchange-rate risk for a transaction.

For example, if a European company wants to import steel from the U.S., it would have to pay for this steel in U.S. dollars. If the price of the euro falls against the dollar before the payment is made, the European company will end up paying more than the original agreement had specified. As such, the European company could enter into a contract to lock in the current exchange rate to eliminate the risk of dealing in U.S. dollars. These contracts could be either forwards or futures contracts.

- Speculators

Another class of participants in forex are the speculators. Instead of hedging against changes in exchange rates or exchanging currency to fund international transactions, speculators attempt to make money by taking advantage of the fluctuating exchange-rate levels.

George Soros is one of the most famous currency speculators. The billionaire hedge fund manager is most famous for speculating on the decline of the British pound, a move that earned $1.1 billion in less than a month. On the other hand, Nick Leeson, a trader with England's Barings Bank, took speculative positions on futures contracts in yen that resulted in losses amounting to more than $1.4 billion, which resulted to the great fall of the entire bank that he worked for. The largest and most controversial speculators on the forex market are hedge funds, which are essentially unregulated funds that use unconventional and often very risky investment strategies to make very large returns. Think of them as mutual funds though without the same level of regulation. Given that they can take such large positions, they can have a major effect on a country's currency and economy at large. Some critics blamed hedge funds for the Asian currency crisis of the late 1990s, while others have pointed to the ineptness of Asian central bankers. Either way, speculators can strongly influence the forex market.

Now that you have a basic understanding of the forex market, its participants and its history, we can move on to some of the more advanced concepts that will bring you closer to being able to make your first currency trade. The next section will look at the main economic theories that underlie the forex market.

CHAPTER FIVE
5.0: PROFITS

5.1: Introduction for the common man.

Profit is the money realized from the sale of goods and services having dealt with the amount used in purchasing the goods initially. It is the financial benefit which is the difference between the amount earned and the amount spent in buying, operating and producing something. It is also the difference between the purchase price and the cost in which it is brought to the market. It could be expressed also as an economic advantage which is really gotten when the amount of revenue earned or gained from a business activity exceeds the expenses, costs and taxes needed to sustain the business's activity. The profit gotten is a gain for the business owner who has a decision to either spend it on the business or on something else – he calls the shot about his profit. This profit determines the economic progress of the business to its owner.

5.2: Introduction for the financial world

Profit in the financial world in the perspective of excess of revenue over cost is the sum of two components: normal profit and economic profit. It is also referred to as the surplus remaining after total costs are deducted from the total revenue, and the basis on which the tax is computed and dividend is paid.

Profit is also income formation in market production-a balance between income generation and income distribution. The income generated is always distributed to the stakeholders of production as economic value within the review interval. The profit is the share of income formation the owner is able to keep to himself/herself in the income distribution process. Profit is one of the major sources of economic well-being because it means incomes and opportunities to develop production. The words income, profit and earnings are substitutes in this context. To accountants, economic profit, or EP, is a single-period metric to determine the value created by a company in one period—usually a year. It is earnings after tax less the equity charge, a risk-weighted cost of capital. This is almost similar to the economists' definition of economic profit.

There are analysts who see the benefit in making adjustments to economic profit such as eliminating the effect of amortized goodwill or capitalizing expenditure on brand advertising to show its value over multiple accounting periods. The underlying concept was first introduced by Eugen Schmalenbach, but the commercial application of the concept of adjusted economic profit was by Stern Stewart & Co. which has trade-marked their adjusted economic profit as Economic Value Added (EVA).

Optimum profit is a theoretical measure and denotes the "right" level of profit a business can achieve. In the business, this figure takes account of marketing strategy, market position, and other methods of increasing returns above the competitive rate.

Accounting profits should include economic profits, which are also called economic rents. For instance, a monopoly can have very high economic profits, and those profits might include a rent on some natural resource that a firm owns, whereby that resource cannot be easily duplicated by other firms.

Calculated as:

Profit = Total Revenue – Total Expenses.

Profit Breakdown.

Profit is the money a business makes after all expenses have accounted. Either the business is a couple of kids running a lemonade stand or a publicly traded multinational company, the aim of every company either a lemonade stand or the multinational company is to consistently make profit As a result, much of the business performance is based on profitability in its various forms. Some analysts are interested in top-line profitability, whereas others are interested in profitability first then expenses, such as taxes and interest, and still others are only concerned with profitability after all expenses have been paid.

There are three major types of profit that an analyst can analyse: gross profit, operating profit and net profit. Each type of profit gives the analyst more information about the company's performance, especially when compared against other time interval and competitors from other investment firms. All three levels of profitability can be found on the income statement.

There are three major types of profit that analysts analyze:

- gross profit
- Operating profit and
- Net profit.

Each type of profit gives the analyst more information about the company's performance, especially when compared against other time periods and industry competitors. All three levels of profitability can be found on the statement of the income.

-Gross, Operating and Net Profit

- The first level of profitably is gross profit. Gross profit is sales minus the cost of goods sold. Sales is the first line item on the income statement and the cost of goods sold, also referred to as CGS and is generally listed just below it. For example, if company A has $100,000 in sales and a CGS of $60,000, it means the gross profit is $100,000 minus $60,000, which is $40,000. Divide gross profit by sales for the gross profit margin, which is $40,000 divided by $100,000, or 40%.

- The second level of profitability is operating profit. Operating profit is calculated by deducting operating expenses from gross profit. Gross profit looks at profitability after direct expenses, and operating profit looks at profitability after operating expenses. These are things like salaries, general and administrative costs, also referred to as SG&A. If company A has $20,000 in operating expenses, the operating profit is $40,000 minus $20,000, equaling $20,000. Divide operating profit by sales for the operating profit margin, which is 20%.

- The third level of profitably is net profit. Net profit is the income left over after all expenses. These includes taxes and interest, having been paid. If interest is $5,000 and taxes are another $5,000, net profit is calculated by deducting both of these from operating profit. In this example the answer is $20,000 minus $5,000, minus $5,000, which equals $10,000. Divide net profit by sales for net profit margin, which is 10%.

What is Gross Profit?

Gross profit is the profit a company makes after removing the costs associated with making and selling its products or the costs attached with the providing of its services. Gross profit will appear on a company's income statement, and can be calculated with this formula:

Gross profit = Revenue - Cost of Goods Sold

Gross profit can also be called sales profit and gross income.

Gross profit assesses a company's efficiency at using its labour and supplies. The parameter only considers variable costs, that is, costs that fluctuate with the level of output, such as:

- materials;
- direct labour, assuming it is hourly or otherwise dependent on output levels;
- commissions for sales staff;
- credit card fees on customer purchases;
- equipment, perhaps including usage-based depreciation;
- utilities for the production site;
- Shipping; etc.

5.3: Gross Profit breakdown

As generally defined, gross profit does not include fixed costs, or costs that must be paid regardless of the level of output. Fixed costs include rent, advertising, insurance, salaries for employees indirectly involved in production, and office supplies. However, it should be noted that a portion of the fixed cost is given to each unit of production under absorption costing, which is required for external reporting under the Generally Accepted Accounting Principles. For example, if a factory produces 10,000 phones in a given period, and the company pays $30,000 in rent for the building, a cost of $3 would be attributed to each phone under costing of absorption.

Gross profit shouldn't be confused with operating profit which is also known as earnings before interest and tax which is the profit a company makes before interest and taxes are factored in. Operating profit is calculated by the subtraction of operating expenses from gross profit.

Gross profit can be used to calculate the gross profit margin. This is expressed as a percentage of revenue, this metric is useful for the comparison of the efficiency in production of a company over time. Simply comparing gross profits from month to month or quarter to quarter can confuse one and cause a misleading. Since gross profits can increase while gross margins decreaase, a worrying trend that could land a company in hot water. The terminology here can cause some confusion: "gross margin" can be used to mean either gross profit or gross profit margin. Gross profit is expressed as a currency value, gross profit margin as a percentage. The formula for gross profit margin is:

Gross profit margin = gross profit / revenue = (revenue - cost of goods sold) / revenue

Gross profit margins differs greatly by industry. Food and beverage stores and construction firms have razor-thin gross profit margins, for example, while the healthcare and banking industries enjoy much larger ones.

Here is an example of how to calculate gross profit and the gross profit margin, using Ford Motor Co.'s 2016 annual income statement:

Revenues	(in USD millions)
Automotive	141,546
Financial services	10,253
Other	1
Total revenues	151,800
Costs and expenses	
Automotive cost of sales	126,584
Selling, administrative, and other expenses	12,196
Financial Services interest, operating, and other expenses	8,904
Total costs and expenses	147,684

To know the gross profit, we first add up the cost of goods sold which sums up to $126,584. We do not include selling, administrative and other expenses, since these are mostly fixed costs. We then subtract the cost of goods sold from revenues to obtain a gross profit of $151,800 - $126,584 = $25,216 million.

To obtain the gross profit margin, we divide the gross profit by total revenues for a margin of $25,216 / $151,800 = 16.61%. This compares favorably to an automotive industry average of around 14%, suggesting that Ford operates more efficiently than its peers.

Standardized income statements prepared by financial data services may give slightly different gross profits. These statements conveniently shows gross profits as a different line item, but are only available for public companies. Investors reviewing private companies' income should familiarize themselves with the cost and expense items on a non-standardized balance sheet that do and don't factor into gross profit calculations.

When investors want to see how a company is performing, chances are they'll browse the company's website or annual report in order to know its income statement. One sees the business's total revenue at the top, followed by several rows of expenses. The very bottom row shows what's remaining which is either the net profit or loss. If this number is bigger than last year's, one might presume the firm is doing better. But is it really?

As it turns out, an organization's performance might be a little more complex than its renowned bottom line. This is why most analysts look at more than one form of profit when evaluating a stock. In addition to the net profit, they may also factor in gross profit which is gross income and operating profit which is operating income. Each of these line items on the income statement has important information about how the company is doing which the investor or depositor knows what to look for, the different measures of profit also aid in the indication of whether the recent trends are good or bad and also if they are likely to continue.

The three major profit.

To understand each type of profit, it's useful to know and at least have a knowledge about the income statement. This is a financial account that shows what the revenue and expenses of the company for a specific time period is, which is most times quarterly or a annually. For a public traded company, an individual can virtually always find it on the company's investors relation webpage

The following is a full-year income statement for Active Tots, a maker of outdoor children's toys.

(in millions)	2012	2011
Net Sales	2,000	1,800
Cost of Goods Sold	(900)	(700)
Gross Profit	1,100	1,100
Operating Expenses (SG&A)	(400)	(250)
Operating Profit	700	850
Other Income (Expense)	(100)	50
Extraordinary Gain (Loss)	400	(100)
Interest Expense	(200)	(150)
Net Profit Before Taxes (Pretax Income)	800	650

Taxes	(250)	(200)
Net Income	550	450

The top line of the table shows the company's revenue or net sales which in other words, all the revenue it has generated over a given stretch of time from its day-to-day operations. From this initial sales figure, the business subtracts all the expenses associated with actually producing its toys, from the raw materials to the wages of people working in its factory. These production-related expenditures are referred to as the "cost of goods sold." The remaining amount, usually on line 3, is the **gross profit**.

The next row down shows the operating expenses of the business which represents selling, general and administrative concepts. Essentially, these are the Overhead. Companies can't just make products and collect the proceeds. They need to hire salespeople who will help to bring the goods to market and executives who help chart the organization's direction. Usually they'll also pay for advertising as well as the cost of any administrative buildings. All of these items are included in the operating expense figure. Once this is subtracted from gross profit, we arrive at the operating profit.

Toward the bottom of the income statement are expenses not related to the firm's core business? An instance is this, there's a line for extraordinary losses and gains, which include events not usual such as the sale of a building or business unit. Here, we also see any gains or losses from investments. Finally, the document includes a line representing the corporation's tax expense. Once these additional expenses are deducted from operating profit, the investor arrives at the net income also known as net profit – or net loss as the case may be. This is the amount of money the company has either added to or subtracted from its coffers over a given time interval.

Understanding the Differences

So why use these different parameters?

Let's examine the Active Tots income statement to find out. Many beginning investors will naturally look right for the net profit line. In this case, the company earned $550 million in its latest fiscal year, up from $450 million the year before.

On the surface, this looks like a positive and a great development. However, taking a closer look reveals some interesting information which as it turns out is that the firm's gross profit, the revenue that remains after subtracting production expenses – is the same from one year to the next. In fact, the cost of goods grew at a faster pace than net sales. There could be any number of reasons for this. Perhaps the cost of plastic, a primary material in many of its products, rose significantly. Or, perhaps, its unionized plant workers negotiated for higher wages.

What is perhaps more interesting is that the business's operating profit actually went down in the latest year. This may be a sign that the company's staff is becoming bloated, or that Active Tots has failed to rein in employee perks or other overhead expenses.

How, then, is the company earning $100 million more in net profit? One of the biggest factors appears toward the bottom of the income statement. Last year, Active Tots recorded an extraordinary $400 million gain. In this case, the one-time windfall was the result of selling its educational products division.

While the sale of this business unit increased net profit, it's not income the company can count on year after year. For this reason, many analysts emphasize operating profit, which really shows the performance of a firm's core business activity, over net profit.

It's important to note, however, that the spending might be positive. An example is if Active Tots saw its operating expenses shoot up as a result of a new advertising campaign, the firm might more than make up for it the following year with increased revenue. In addition to looking at the income statement, it's Germaine to read up on the company to find out the reason for the change in figures.

Evaluating Performance

Profit metrics can help assess a company's health in two ways. The first is to use them for an internal review – in other words, new numbers are compared to the firm's historical data. A knowledgeable investor will look for trends that help predict future performance. For instance, if the costs associated with production have risen faster than the company's sales over multiple years, it may be difficult for the company to maintain healthy profit margins going forward. By contrast, if its administrative performance start to take up a smaller part of revenue, the company is probably doing some belt-tightening that will enhance profitability.

Investors should also compare these three parameters which are the gross profit, operating profit and net profit – to those of a company's competitors. Many investors look at what is earned per figures, which are based on net profit, when deciding which stocks offer the best value. However, because one-time gains or expenses can scatter the financial activity or performance, many securities analyst will instead key in on operating profit to determine what shares are worth.

The Bottom Line

While it's tempting to look at the bottom line of an income statement to size up a company, investors should be careful and not negligent of the fact of this figure's shortcomings. Because gross profit and operating profit place a focus on the company's core activities, these numbers are often the best standard one can use in determining an organization's future course.

What is 'Net Profit Margin'

Net profit margin is the ratio of net profits to revenues generated for a company or business segment. Typically expressed as a percentage, net profit margins show how much of each dollar collected by a company as revenue translates into profit. The equation to calculate net profit margin is: net margin = net profit / revenue.

'Net Profit Margin' breakdown.

Net margins vary from organisation to orgnisation, and certain ranges can be expected in certain industries, as similar business constraints exist in each distinct industry. Low profit margins don't necessarily equate to low profits. For example, Wal-Mart Stores Inc. has delivered high returns for its shareholders while operating on net margins less than 5% annually. In fact, in the first quarter of 2016, Walmart's profit margin was 2.66%. In contrast, a business with very small operating budget such as an independent contractor working as a freelance writer has a very small overhead and as a result, most of its revenue is tied to profits. However, although freelance writing may have a high profit margin, its annual profits may seem low in comparison with a multinational corporation such as Walmart.

Most publicly traded companies report their net margins both quarterly during earnings releases and in their reports for each year. Companies that are able to expand their net margins over time are generally rewarded with share price growth, as share price growth leads directly to higher levels of profitability.

How to Calculate Net Profit Margin?

To calculate net profit margin, know what the company's revenue is, which consists of all the sales, fees or other money the business has collected through the period. To ascertain profits, subtract operating expenses, cost of goods sold, interest and tax from revenue. If the business pays stock dividends, also subtract those payments from revenue when calculating profit, but do not take common stock dividends into account. Then, simply divide net profit by revenue, and to convert that number into a percent, multiply it by 100.

To illustrate, imagine a business has $100,000 in revenue, but it also has $20,000 in operating costs, $10,000 in cost of goods sold and $14,000 in tax liability. Its net profits are $56,000. Profits divided by revenue equals .56 or 56%. A 56% profit margin indicates the company earns 56 cents in profit for every dollar it collects.

The Importance of Net Profit Margins

Net profit margin is one of the most important indicators of a business's financial health. It can give a more accurate view of how profitable a business is than its cash flow, and by tracking increases and decreases in its net profit margin, a business can assess whether or not current practices are working. Additionally, because net profit margin is expressed as a percentage rather than a dollar amount, as net profit is, it makes it possible to compare the profitability of two or more businesses regardless of their differences in size. Finally, a business can use its net profit margin to forecast profits based on revenues.

What is 'Operating Profit'

Operating profit is an accounting figure that measures the profit earned from a company's ongoing core business operations, thus excluding deductions of interest and taxes. This value also does not include any profit earned from the firm's investments, such as earnings from firms in which the company has partial interest.

Operating profit can be calculated using the following formula:

Operating Profit = Operating Revenue - Cost of Goods Sold – operating expenses - Depreciation – Amortization

'Operating Profit' breakdown

Operating profit serves as an indicator of the business's potential profitability with all extraneous factors removed from the calculation. All expenses that are necessary to keep the business running are included, which is why operating profit does take into account asset-related depreciation and amortization which are accounting tools that result from a firm's operations. Operating profit is therefore distinct from the net income, which differs from year to year due to these exceptions in a firm's operating profit.

Operating profit is also sometimes referred to as operating income, as well as earnings before interest and tax — although the latter may sometimes include non-operating revenue which is not a part of operating profit. If a firm does not have non-operating revenue, its operating profit will equal earnings before interest and tax.

Given the formulas for gross income (Revenue – cost of goods sold), the formula for operating profit is often simplified as: Gross Profit - Operating Expenses – depreciation - amortization.

Exclusions from the Operating Profit Calculation

Revenue created through the sale of assets, outside of those assets created for the purpose of being sold as part of the core business, are not included in the operating profit figure. Additionally, interest earned through mechanisms such as checking or money market accounts are not included.

While the removal of production cost from overall operating revenue, along with any costs associated with depreciation and amortization, are permitted when determining the operating profit, the calculation does not account for any debt obligations that must be met even if those obligations are directly tied to the company's ability to maintain normal business operations.

Operating income does not include investment income generated through a partial stake in another company even if the investment income in question is tied directly to the core business operations of the second company. Additionally, the sale of assets such as real estate and production equipment are not included as these sales are not a part of the core operations of the business.

An Example of Operating Profit

Walmart Inc. reported operating income of $20.4 billion for its fiscal year 2018. Total revenues, which were equal to total operating revenues, tallied $500.3 billion. These revenues came from sales across Walmart's global umbrella of physical stores, including Sam's Club, and e-commerce businesses. Meanwhile, the cost of sales (or COGS) and operating, selling, general and administrative expenses, totalled $373.4 billion and $106.5 billion, respectively. The firm did not separately list amortization and depreciation on its income statement.

- OR [$500.3 billion] - COGS [$373.4 billion] - OE [$106.5 billion] = Operating Profit [$20.4 billion]

From the $20.4 billion, net income further subtracted interest expenses of $2.2 billion, a loss on extinguishment of debt totalling $3.1 billion and a provision for income taxes of $4.6 billion, for a net income total of $10.5 billion.

Benefits and Drawbacks of Referring to the Operating Profit Figure

Companies may choose to present their operating profit figures, in lieu of their net profit figures, as the net profit of a company contains the effects of interest payments and taxes. In cases where a company has a particularly high debt load, the operating profit may present the company's financial situation more positively than the net profit reflects.

For investors, examining the operating profit may allow for an easier comparison of businesses that operate within industries with differing tax rates or financial structures as this allows for a more equitable comparison.

While positive operating profit may express the overall profit potential of a business, it does not guarantee the business is not experiencing losses. A company with a high debt load may show a positive operating profit while also having a negative net profit. Additionally, large but extraneous costs are not represented, which can again show a company with a negative net profit as having a positive operating profit.

To calculate gross profit margin, subtract the cost of goods sold from a company's revenue; then divide by revenue. If a company sells goods for $100 and pays $70 to produce those goods, the company's gross profit margin is 30%.

To calculate net profit margin, take the gross profit and subtract operating and all other expenses, such as taxes and interest paid on debt. Then divide by revenue. If the same company has operating expenses, taxes and interest totalling $20, its net profit margin is 10%.

While gross profit margin provides a general indication of profitability, net profit margin is a more accurate measure. Increases in revenue do not necessarily create increases in profitability. Net profit margin reveals the percentage of revenue that reflects a company's profit per dollar of sales.

Let's face it, a company's most important goal is to make money and keep it, which depends on liquidity and efficiency. Because these characteristics determine a company's ability to pay investors a dividend, profitability is reflected in share price. As such, investors should know how to analyze various facets of profitability, including how efficiently a company uses its resources and how much income it generates from operations. Calculating a company's profit margin is a great way to gain insight into these and other aspects of how well a company generates and retains money.

Why Use Profit-Margin Ratios?

The bottom line is the first thing many investors look at to gauge a company's profitability. It's awfully tempting to rely on net earnings alone to gauge profitability, but it doesn't always provide a clear picture of the company, and using it as the sole measure of profitability can have big repercussions.

Profit-margin ratios, on the other hand, can give investors deeper insight into management efficiency. But instead of measuring how much managers earn from assets, equity or invested capital, these ratios measure how much money a company squeezes from its total revenue or total sales.

Margins, quite simply, are earnings expressed as a ratio, or a percentage of sales. A percentage allows investors to compare the profitability of different companies, while net earnings, which are presented as an absolute number, cannot.

For example, suppose that Company A had an annual net income of $749 million on sales of about $11.5 billion last year. Its major competitor, Company B, earned about $990 million for the year on sales of about $19.9 billion. Comparing Company B's net earnings of $990 million to Company A's $749 million shows that Company B earned more than Company A, but it doesn't tell you very much about profitability. If you look at the net profit margin, or the earnings generated from each dollar of sales, you'll see that Company A produced 6.5 cents on each dollar of sales, while Company returned less than 5 cents.

There are three key profit-margin ratios: gross profit margins, operating profit margins and net profit margins.

Gross Profit Margin

The gross profit margin tells us the profit a company makes on its cost of sales, or cost of goods sold. In other words, it indicates how efficiently management uses labour and supplies in the production process.

$$\text{Gross Profit Margin} = (\text{Sales} - \text{Cost of Goods Sold})/\text{Sales}$$

Suppose that a company has $1 million in sales and the cost of its labour and materials amounts to $600,000. Its gross margin rate would be 40% ($1 million - $600,000/$1 million).

Companies with high gross margins will have a lot of money left over to spend on other business operations, such as research and development or marketing, so be on the lookout for downward trends in the gross margin rate over time. This is a sign of future problems facing the bottom line. When labour and material costs increase rapidly, they are likely to lower gross profit margins - unless, of course, the company can pass these costs onto customers in the form of higher prices.

It's important to remember that gross profit margins can vary drastically from business to business and from industry to industry. For instance, the airline industry has a gross margin of about 5%, while the software industry has a gross margin of about 90%.

Operating Profit Margin

By comparing earnings before interest and taxes to sales, operating profit margins show how successful a company's management has been at generating income from the operation of the business:

$$\text{Operating Profit Margin} = \text{Earnings before interest and tax}/\text{Sales}$$

If EBIT amounted to $200,000 and sales equalled $1 million, the operating profit margin would be 20%.

This ratio is a rough measure of the operating leverage a company can achieve in the conduct of the operational part of its business. It indicates how much earnings before interest and tax is generated per dollar of sales. High operating profits can mean the company has effective control of costs, or that sales are increasing faster than operating costs.

Operating profit also gives investors an opportunity to do profit-margin comparisons between companies that do not issue a separate disclosure of their cost of goods sold figures (which are needed to do gross margin analysis). Operating profit measures how much cash the business throws off, and some consider it a more reliable measure of profitability since it is harder to manipulate with accounting tricks than net earnings.

Naturally, because the operating profit margin accounts for not only costs of materials and labour, but also administration and selling costs, it should be a much smaller figure than the gross margin.

Net Profit Margin

Net profit margins are those generated from all phases of a business, including taxes. In other words, this ratio compares net income with sales. It comes as close as possible to summing-up in a single figure how effectively managers run the business:

$$\text{Net Profit Margins} = \text{Net Profits after Taxes}/\text{Sales}$$

If a company generates after-tax earnings of $100,000 on its $1 million of sales, then its net margin amounts to 10%.

To be comparable from company to company and from year to year, net profits after tax must be shown before minority interests have been deducted and equity income added. Not all companies have these items. In addition, investment income, which is wholly dependent upon the whims of management, can change dramatically from year to year.

Again, just like gross and operating profit margins, net margins vary between industries. By comparing a company's gross and net margins, we can get a good sense of its non-production and non-direct costs like administration, finance and marketing costs.

For example, the international airline industry has a gross margin of just 5%. Its net margin is just a tad lower, at about 4%. On the other hand, discount airline companies have much higher gross and net margin numbers. These differences provide some insight into these industries' distinct cost structures: compared to its bigger, international cousins, the discount airline industry spends proportionately more on things like finance, administration and marketing, and proportionately less on items such as fuel and flight crew salaries.

In the software business, gross margins are very high, while net profit margins are considerably lower. This shows that marketing and administration costs in this industry are very high, while cost of sales and operating costs are relatively low.

When a company has a high profit margin, it usually means that it also has one or more advantages over its competition. Companies with high net profit margins have a bigger cushion to protect themselves during the hard times. Companies with low profit margins can get wiped out in a downturn. And companies with profit margins reflecting a competitive advantage are able to improve their market share during the hard times - leaving them even better positioned when things improve again.

In summary

Margin analysis is a great way to understand the profitability of companies. It tells us how effectively management can wring profits from sales, and how much room a company has to withstand a downturn, fend off competition and make mistakes. But, like all ratios, margin ratios never offer perfect information. They are only as good as the timeliness and accuracy of the financial data that gets fed into them, and analysing them also depends on a consideration of the company's industry and its position in the business cycle.

Remember, margin ratios highlight companies that are worth further examination. Knowing that a company has a gross margin of 25% or a net profit margin of 5% tells us very little without further information. As with any ratio used on its own, margins tell us a lot, but not the whole story, about a company's prospects.

. 5.5: How Profit can be or is made by using different financial strategies during the Bear Market

The following ways are Put Options of Financial strategies in which Profit is made during the Bear Market;

1. Finding profitable trading strategies during a bear market is often challenging. Experienced traders, however, can use option contracts to profit in almost any economy or market situation. One options traders profit in a down market involves employing the use of put options. Whether the contract is purchased for protection, called a hedge, or sold as a play on falling prices, a put option has several advantages in a bear market when used correctly.

2. Hedging Downside Risk: Conservative options traders can use put options in a bear market to protect against losses on a position they currently own, this is known as a long position. For example, if a trader owns 100 shares of ABC stock at a price of $50 per share, he or she can purchase a put option with a strike price of $55 as a form of insurance on the investment. In this scenario, if the stock price in a bear market moves below $50, the trader can exercise the put option, capturing a price higher than the market and securing a $5-per-share profit. Granted, the purchase price of the put option, called the premium, needs to be factored into the net profit calculation.

3. Lowering Acquisition Costs with Naked Puts: A riskier trade with potentially high profits, called a naked put, is another trading strategy to use in bear market trading. Not only do traders have the opportunity to pocket a nice premium from the sale of such puts, they can use this strategy to acquire shares of a stock at a great price. Say ABC stock is trading at $50 and falling in a bear market. The trader can sell a put contract, equal to 100 shares of the underlying stock, with a strike price of $40 and collect a nice premium. If the price falls below $40, the put is likely to be exercised, meaning the trader is obligated to purchase 100 shares of ABC at $40. His or her total cost for the shares is adjusted to include the premium collected, making this strategy a nice way to obtain stock at lower prices. The key to this trade's profitability lies with the likelihood the stock turns around and can be sold at a higher price later.

4. Proceed with Caution: Bear markets can take a toll on portfolios, so finding a way to make money in the meantime by selling put options can seem like a worthwhile trading strategy. In reality, as bear markets, or any market for that matter, are unpredictable, traders should only consider selling puts on stocks they would not ultimately mind owning. Likewise, consider strike prices only if you see value at that price. A strategy to collect only premiums as profit is much easier and safer to accomplish through selling covered calls, especially during a bear market.

5.6: Why x/y/z does or does not make profit during the financial downturn

Even in a recession, you can find clever ways to extract economic advantage and position yourself for the next economic recovery. Not all times are good, but if you want to lead a wealthy life, then you would be wise to learn how to find the good in every situation. That includes the bad times associated with an economic downturn.

The following six ways helps you to make profit during a market downturn

1. Lower your Costs: Whether you're running a business or running a household, now is the time to cut costs and become a lean, mean, cash flow machine. Eliminate redundant employees and get marginal employees with better quality from the plentiful job market. Also, find lower-cost providers for services and goods, and cut every form of

waste and fat. When you waste nothing and use every resource to its maximum advantage, it's good for the environment and even better for your bottom line. Now that business is slowing down, use that extra time to lower your costs and improve quality and efficiency and at the same time reducing or removing irrelevances.

2. Own Instead of Rent: With fall in real estate price, and interest rates low, it may make sense to purchase your office or home rather than renew the lease. The economic relationship of rent versus own has changed dramatically in the last two years. Most accountants agree that if your time horizon for using the real estate extends to 20 years or more, the scales will usually tilt in favor of ownership. Check it out.

3. Bargain Shop: Many vendors are offering steep price concessions. It seems everyone is having a sale, but you have to ask for the discount. You'll be amazed by how much money you can save just by asking for a discount. You can check it out for a week.

4. Add to Your Portfolio: The best time to build your portfolio is when investments are beaten down and valuations are strong. There's an inverse correlation between long-term investment returns and the valuations of the market at the time you acquired your portfolio. The lowest valuations have the highest expected returns. Build your portfolio when securities are "on sale."

5. Refinance Debt: Interest rates are bouncing off historic lows. I recently refinanced my home with a 4.75% 30-year fixed rate loan… unbelievable, right? At that rate, I can't ever imagine wanting to pay it off. My investment returns greatly exceeded that rate and inflation is highly likely to approach or exceed that rate over the lifetime of the loan. What that means is they're effectively paying me to borrow the money when they offer rates that low. Locking down unrealistically low, long-term, fixed rate mortgages is an extraordinary opportunity in today's recessionary environment. This is one of my favorites. This strategy applies to investment real estate as well as your personal residence. The key is it must be a fully amortizing, long-term, fixed rate loan. No balloons, variables or other hybrid loans are allowed.

6. Take Advantage of Government Boondoggles: I personally despise all the government bailout and incentive programs. There's no reason the taxpayer should be going deeper into debt to encourage consumers to purchase cars (Cash for Clunkers) or homes (First Time Home Buyers Tax Credit). However, like it or not, these industries are favored by the government. If you're already in the market for a car or first home, only a fool wouldn't take such an advantage of these government handouts. Don't respond to these incentives by creating demand but rather do use them if you were already considering a purchase. I may hate the game but as long as the music is playing you should be smart and do the dance.

CONCLUSION

Market has treated earlier faces a lot of challenges; no matter how flourishing it may look, there are times when challenges will be faced -market downturn. However, every business requires risk to be taken even knowing the outcome will be favorable. Whenever there is a market downturn, there is need to be optimistic; be hopeful because there is always a market rebound. Whatever happens in a market doesn't stay for long, one would only hope it doesn't take long for a market turnaround.

In conclusion, the goal of every market is to be successful and the objectives would be a guide to fulfilling such dreams.

www.ingramcontent.com/pod-product-compliance
Lightning Source LLC
Chambersburg PA
CBHW030500220526
45464CB00006B/2587